As someone who prefers expanded snacks for dinner, this book is exactly what I want to eat. Mix & Match Potato Bites? Yes, please. Burrata with Fruit, Pesto, and Crostini? Sign me up! I want to live in these pages full of colorful produce and gorgeous tablescapes. Can't wait to cook my way through this book!

ERIN GLEESON, artist and NYT bestselling author of *The Forest Feast*

As a parent to growing teens, I struggle with dinner ideas that meet my kids' expanding palates, evolving appetites, and wild schedules—all while feeding myself well, too! With creative recipes in a variety of "snacking styles" and its gorgeous photographs, *Snacking Dinners* has my family saying: "Let's make THAT for dinner!"

SARAH POWERS, co-host of *The Mom Hour* podcast and co-author of *The Mother's Gratitude Journal: An Easy Guide to Capturing Everyday Joys and Milestone Moments*

Finally, permission to snack for dinner! And why not? As Georgia Freedman proves, dinners assembled from favorite nibbles are fun, versatile, satisfying, and best of all, easy. Here is a cookbook tailor-made for people with busy lives who also love good food. Sign me up!

EMMA CHRISTENSEN, Simply Recipes and The Spruce Eats

SNACKING DINNERS

50+ Recipes for Low-Lift, High-Reward
Dinners That Delight

Georgia Freedman

PHOTOGRAPHS
Leela Cyd

Hardie Grant

NORTH AMERICA

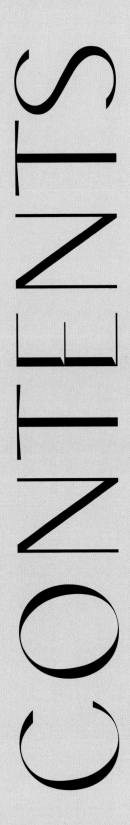

CONTENTS

CLASSIC SNACKS & VARIATIONS

PREP-AHEAD SNACKS

SPLURGY SNACKS

INTRODUCTION

Ask me what I want to eat when I have a night to myself—a night I can take a step back from the demands of family life and make something *just for me*—and the picture I'll paint is a meal that is all delight and zero obligation. What I want, really, is an expanded snack: something that is easy to throw together, full of my favorite flavors, and, most importantly, fun to eat. Rich sardines with zingy pickled chiles on crackers. Perfectly ripe summer fruit with creamy burrata to pile on crostini. Chilled tofu slices topped with fresh tomatoes and crunchy chile crisp. These meals feel like a respite from the pressures of the world.

While this type of low-lift, high-reward meal has recently been refreshed under the "girl dinner" trend, snacking meals have always been the secret weapon of busy people, from professionals who get home too late (and too tired) to stand over a stove to moms who need to get dinner ready fast (and make it fun). They are endlessly versatile and accommodating to any food preference and can be scaled up and down easily, all of which makes them as perfect for a solo eater as they are for a large family. They're really kind of magical in their simplicity and promise—something every cook, whether they're a "girlie" or not, should have in their repertoire.

People who love a grazing-style meal know that a good one can be far more than random odds and ends from the fridge. If you stock your kitchen with ingredients you love, a "snack" can be an opportunity to treat yourself to your favorite flavors. It can also offer a chance to enjoy splurgy ingredients you wouldn't buy in large quantities, like a wedge of really good cheese, a slice of rich pâté, or a single serving of freshly picked crabmeat.

Snacking meals can be a thoughtful, intentional way to use up leftovers (quickly frying day-old rice for a crispy Thai-inspired salad, for instance). They can also be something you plan for and prep in advance, doing easy steps like roasting vegetables so you can have an indulgent treat when you're tired at the end of the day. At its core, a snacking dinner is about quickly assembling ingredients to make something delightful.

My definition of what makes a snacking dinner is broad. It encompasses fancied-up versions of treats you might have eaten after school as a kid as well as dishes found on the appetizer side of the menu or the small plates served at a wine bar.

The recipes I'm sharing here include classic snacks that have been expanded into meals and other dishes I have reimagined and snackified. They reflect traditions and flavors from across the globe. They include dips and things to spread on crackers, things in wraps, and things assembled beautifully on boards. Most are finger foods—because anything you can eat with your hands feels more fun.

Some of these recipes involve a little cooking, and a few also ask you to make something ahead of time so that it's waiting for you in your fridge. Others don't require you to do anything but assemble ingredients on a plate and maybe add a little seasoning or mix up a quick dressing. Some are made with ingredients you can find easily in any Western supermarket; others take full advantage of the incredible Asian, Middle Eastern, Latinx, and African grocery stores you can now find in most cities and the wealth of online vendors. Some are extremely nutritious; others are less so (not every night needs to be about salad and a light protein).

Several of these recipes make for relatively small dinners—especially the ones made with rich ingredients that are too heavy for large portions. To round out your dinner, I've included suggestions for simple-to-prepare or premade additions like chips, crudités, and jammy boiled eggs.

Each recipe in this book is designed to feed one because I'd like to encourage you to make flavorful, delightful meals for yourself whenever you want something fun. I find that many of us only take the time to make an interesting dinner if we're feeding someone else—even if we enjoy cooking, our best efforts go to treating our friends, partners, and other loved ones. But I firmly believe that you should give yourself just as much care and attention as you give others. For me, that starts with taking the time to feed myself as well as I would feed someone else at my table (while also letting myself off the hook about what it means to "cook" dinner every night).

That said, when you do want to cook for others, these meals are perfect for sharing. Double them, and they make for a low-lift date night. Put them in front of a kid, and dinner becomes an adventure. Arrange a few different snacks on the table together, and you've got an instant party (see page 10 for some of my favorite combos). Just as making something fun for yourself shouldn't be a chore, caring for the other people in your life—or even throwing a party—doesn't have to wear you out.

However you use these recipes, I hope they inspire you to make nourishing yourself a priority and offer you opportunities to add a few moments of pure fun and delight to your week.

SHARING YOUR SNACKS

While the recipes in this book are designed for one, snacking dinners are also ideal for groups of all kinds. You can use them to plan a fun and easy date night, pull them out when a friend drops by, or use them to make dinnertime fun for the whole family. **All these recipes can be doubled (or tripled or quadrupled),** and recipes like Make-Your-Own Spicy Tuna Hand Rolls (page 65), the Antipasti Board with Roasted Artichoke Hearts (page 66), and the Spiced Nuts, Olives, and Raisins on Hummus (page 107) make a meal feel like a party when you gather a few people around the table. (If you double—or quadruple—any of the recipes, be aware that the prep and cook times will probably be a bit longer.)

My favorite approach to a snacking meal for a couple or a crowd, however, is to make a variety of different snacks that work together as a themed meal. Here are some of my favorite combos.

OLD-SCHOOL STEAKHOUSE BAR

Shrimp Cocktail with Citrus-Gochujang Seafood Sauce (page 93); Zuni-Inspired Celery Sticks (page 22)

Add-ons: High-quality kettle-cooked potato chips and salted nuts

MIDDLE EAST IN CALIFORNIA

Spiced Nuts, Olives, and Raisins on Hummus (page 107); Deconstructed Winter Fruit Fattoush (page 117)

Add-ons: Store-bought stuffed grape leaves and assorted olives

TOKYO NIGHTS

Okonomiyaki Tater Tots (page 62) with optional celery salad add-on; Make-Your-Own Spicy Tuna Hand Rolls (page 65)

Add-ons: Wasabi peas and Amanoya Himemaru Japanese rice crackers

MOVIE NIGHT

Spiced Popcorn Three Ways (page 56); Chorizo and Black Bean Nachos (page 85)

Add-ons: Extra-large box of Raisinets, M&Ms, or other movie theater candy

AFTER-SCHOOL SNACKS

Apple Slices and Cheddar with Crackers and Jam (page 75); Deconstructed Guacamole (page 17); Grown-up "PB&J" Rice Crackers (page 55)

Add-ons: Ritz peanut butter sandwich crackers and Girl Scout Cookies

SICHUAN SNACK STREET

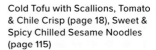

Cold Tofu with Scallions, Tomato & Chile Crisp (page 18), Sweet & Spicy Chilled Sesame Noodles (page 115)

Add-ons: Pan-fried dumplings (from frozen) and 50Hertz Tingly Sichuan Pepper Peanuts

GAME NIGHT

Sweet-Spicy-Numbing Queso (page 79); Mix & Match Potato Bites (page 104); Roti Pizza (page 33)

Add-ons: Root beer floats

GARDEN PARTY

Crudités with Yogurt-Miso Green Goddess Dip (page 80); Pimento Cheese and Tomato Finger Sandwiches (page 97); Burrata with Fruit, Pesto & Crostini (page 25)

Add-ons: Shortbread cookies

TRIP TO MADRID

Conservas with Pan con Tomate (page 52); Spanish Tuna, Tomato & Olive Salad (page 27); Salt & Spice Jammy Eggs (page 71)

Add-ons: Spanish potato chips

PANTRY PICNIC

Sardines with Pickled Peppers (page 48); Spiced Popcorn Three Ways (page 56); Black Bean Picadillo with Chips (page 61)

Add-ons: Assorted dried fruits and cookies—whatever's available!

FRESH & FAST SNACKS

Soft cheese and fresh fruit. Tangy salads wrapped up in cabbage leaves. Crispy flatbreads topped with a whisper of tomato and lots of bright herbs. These are the snacks we crave when we want something fun and delicious for dinner but don't want to spend much time hovering over a stove. They rely on the flavors of a few delicious ingredients and don't require much work to get on the table. Some come together in a couple of minutes with just a bit of chopping; others require a quick blitz of a food processor or a pan shoved under the broiler. None take longer than twenty minutes, give or take, and some take far less time.

These recipes sometimes involve a little planning ahead so that you can make a trip to the store for fresh ingredients, but the easy treats they make are more than enough of a reward. Sit down with them and you'll want to slow down, focus on your plate, and enjoy your meal, bite by bite.

MEAL-WORTHY TOASTS

Toast, open-faced sandwich, smørrebrød, tartine—call it whatever you like, but crisping bread and piling on some delicious ingredients is one of the fastest, easiest ways to make a satisfying meal. Here are some ideas to get you started on your next toast adventure; feel free to use whatever bread you have available or the options I've suggested here.

1 THE ELVIS

Toppings: Peanut butter, sliced bananas, and crumbled bacon on white bread

Vibe: Fit for the King

2 WHITE & GREEN

Toppings: Ricotta, peas, and soft herbs on rustic whole wheat

Vibe: Spring on a plate

3 CHA CHAAN TENG MEETS KOPITIAM

Toppings: Chopped soft-boiled egg on fluffy milk bread drizzled with sweetened condensed milk and a splash of soy sauce

Vibe: Hopping a flight from Hong Kong to Singapore

4 CLASSIC SMØRREBRØD

Toppings: Butter, pickled herring, sliced onion, and dill on Danish rye

Vibe: Fishing village in Denmark

5 PLOUGHMAN'S FEAST

Toppings: An almost unwieldy pile of sharp cheddar, ham, and maybe some bits of chopped cornichon on crusty bread spread with whole-grain mustard and apricot jam

Vibe: A full pub lunch in every bite

6 UNI & ROE

Toppings: Freshly shucked uni and caviar or salmon roe on milk bread with a squeeze of lemon and a sprinkling of thinly sliced chives

Vibe: Mermaid's kiss

7 CLASSIC AVOCADO

Toppings: Thinly sliced avocado, pickled onions, good olive oil, and flaky sea salt on a sliced boule

Vibe: California morning

8 TOMATO MELT

Toppings: Fresh tomato slices topped with melted cheddar on sourdough

Vibe: Soup with grilled cheese, but make it toast

9 THE UPPER WEST SIDE

Toppings: Cream cheese, lox, and capers on rye

Vibe: Forgot to buy bagels

DECONSTRUCTED GUACAMOLE

1 large, thick-skinned avocado (like Hass or Gem)

2 big lemon wedges

Extra-virgin olive oil

Flaky salt

2 or 3 cherry or grape tomatoes

A few cilantro leaves

Tortilla chips

This simple snack is a California classic. When I was a teenager, I made it after school as a quick pick-me-up, cutting open a ripe avocado, seasoning it with some lemon and salt, and scooping up big bites with a spoon or some sturdy tortilla chips (or those thick corn chips that were so popular in the '80s). It wasn't until years later that I realized I was essentially eating a big serving of very basic guacamole without the fuss of mashing everything together. This same idea makes an excellent centerpiece for a snacking dinner.

Halve the avocado and remove the pit. Hold one half in your palm, flesh up, and use the tip of a paring knife to gently cut the flesh lengthwise into thick segments and then crosswise into squares, cutting to the avocado skin but not through it. Run the knife along the inside of the skin to loosen the flesh. Repeat with the other half.

Squeeze some lemon juice into each half. Drizzle on some olive oil and sprinkle on a pinch of salt. Gently squeeze the avocado to open up the cuts in the flesh so the seasonings can make their way between the pieces.

Halve or quarter the tomatoes and finely chop the cilantro then divide both between the avocado halves. To eat, use chips to scoop the avocado directly out of its skin, grabbing some tomato and cilantro with each bite.

Bulk Up the Plate: To fill out your snacking plate, pile more cherry tomatoes on the side along with some carrot slices; if you want more protein, scoop some cottage cheese onto the plate and cover it in more of the toppings.

COLD TOFU WITH SCALLIONS, TOMATO & CHILE CRISP

1 scallion, white and light-green parts only

1 handful cherry tomatoes, or ½ small, flavorful tomato

Cucumber (Chinese, English, or Persian; optional)

8 ounces (225 g) high-quality silken tofu

2 teaspoons Chinese light soy sauce

1 teaspoon Chinese black vinegar

½ teaspoon chile crisp

¼ teaspoon toasted sesame oil

Toasted sesame seeds

Tofu has a gentle flavor and is both light and satisfying. This dish enhances that flavor with just a hint of soy sauce, vinegar, and sesame. It also highlights tofu's cooling properties by adding a little heat from jarred chile crisp, for contrast. Chopped tomato rounds out the mix of subtle, delicious flavors.

Halve the scallion lengthwise and then cut it very thinly crosswise; put it in a small bowl of cold water to mellow. Roughly chop the tomato(es) and thinly slice the cucumber, if using.

Drain the tofu, gently flip it out of the package and onto a plate, and cut it into thick slices. Dress the tofu with the soy sauce, vinegar, chile crisp, and sesame oil, making sure to drizzle each one over every slice of tofu, so the liquid can seep between each piece. Drain the scallion and sprinkle it and the pieces of tomato on top of the tofu. Scatter a couple big pinches of sesame seeds on top. Add the cucumber to the side of the plate, if using.

Bulk Up the Plate: For a heartier meal, make some short-grain rice, add some boiled or spiced peanuts and a handful of steamed edamame, or make some pan-fried dumplings (the kind that can be cooked right out of the freezer).

SWEET POTATO CHIP "SALAD" WITH HOT HONEY & FRESH HERBS

¼ cup (65 g) plain yogurt

¼ cup (35 g) crumbled feta

½ to 1 teaspoon freshly squeezed lemon juice

½ teaspoon extra-virgin olive oil

½ teaspoon garlic powder

Kosher salt

1 scallion, white and light-green parts only

¼ cup packed (8 g) cilantro leaves and thin stems

1 tablespoon dill fronds and thin stems

4 teaspoons hot honey (or 3 teaspoons honey and 1 teaspoon chile crisp)

One 5-ounce (140 g) bag of thick-cut sweet potato chips, such as Terra brand

Za'atar

This dish has a bit of an identity crisis. It's kind of like chips and dip, but the flavors are reminiscent of roast sweet potato wedges with herbs, and the whole thing is plated like a salad—a crunchy one you eat with your fingers. The earthy sweet potato is a perfect vehicle for a tart dip-like dressing of feta, yogurt, and lemon, and lots of fresh herbs lift and brighten the flavors and give the dish its salad-like feel. A final drizzle of sweet-spicy hot honey (or a mix of honey and chile crisp) makes the whole thing irresistible.

Smash the yogurt and feta together in a small bowl, leaving some of the feta in clumps. Stir in the lemon juice, olive oil, garlic powder, and a big pinch of salt; adjust the seasonings to taste. Cut the scallion in half lengthwise and then very thinly crosswise; finely chop the cilantro and dill. If you're making your own hot honey, mix the honey and chile crisp in a small dish and set aside.

Put about half the sweet potato chips on a large plate in an even layer. Drizzle them with half the yogurt dressing and half the hot honey, then sprinkle on half the scallion, cilantro, and dill and a couple big pinches of za'atar. Repeat with a second layer of chips and the remaining ingredients.

Bulk Up the Plate: To add more protein to this meal, try it with a Saturday Bagel jammy egg (page 71); a side of pickles would also work well.

ZUNI-INSPIRED CELERY STICKS

3 large celery sticks

One 2¼-ounce (64 g) piece of Parmesan

3 small or 1½ large anchovies

4 pitted kalamata olives

2 teaspoons extra-virgin olive oil

2 teaspoons mayonnaise

1 big lemon wedge

¾ teaspoon yuzu kosho (optional)

Flat-leaf parsley, for garnish

The most famous dish at San Francisco's much-loved Zuni Café is its roast chicken. But ask regulars what they order time and time again, and a different item might come out on top: the appetizer plate of house-cured anchovies with celery, Parmesan, and olives. This simple combination of ingredients—served in rows on a plate, drizzled with olive oil—is so popular that it never leaves the menu. Here, I used those same ingredients but made them easier to eat by piling them into celery boats. I also add a little zing by stirring in a touch of spicy yuzu kosho (which I, personally, think really brings all the flavors together).

Trim the ends of the celery sticks and use a vegetable peeler to remove the outer skin and strings, then cut each stick in half widthwise to make shorter lengths. Grate the Parmesan on a box grater (you should have about a lightly packed cup). Mince the anchovies and two of the olives, then combine them in a small bowl with the Parmesan, olive oil, and mayonnaise. Squeeze in the juice from the lemon wedge and add the yuzu kosho, if using, then mash the ingredients with the back of a fork so that everything kind of holds together. (If you have a few minutes, refrigerating the mixture will help it stick together.) Fill the celery sticks with the cheese mixture, then chop the remaining two olives and use them and the parsley to garnish.

Bulk Up the Plate: Since this is basically built like an old-school steakhouse bar snack, pair it with other bar nibbles like good-quality potato chips and a bowl of spiced nuts.

BURRATA WITH FRUIT, PESTO & CROSTINI

⅓ of a baguette

¼ cup (60 ml) pesto, homemade (recipe follows) or store-bought

½ teaspoon red wine vinegar

Extra-virgin olive oil

One 4½-ounce (130 g) ball of burrata

Assorted very ripe fruit (ideally a mix, such as 1 peach, 1 or 2 apricots, some figs, and a few cherries)

Honey

Flaky sea salt

Hot summer evenings practically beg for snacking dinners that you can get on the table without ever turning on the stove. This simple combination is the perfect answer; it doesn't require anything other than a food processor (or some premade pesto) and a good knife, but it's elegant enough to feel really special. By pairing creamy burrata with an assortment of sweet fresh fruit, and then drizzling it all with a quick pesto-based sauce, you can get all the sweet, bright, sharp, and creamy flavors into one bite. Eat this with some sliced baguette, toasted or not. This works equally well with fall fruit like figs, soft pears, sliced red grapes, and even jellylike pieces of Hachiya persimmon.

Cut the baguette into ½-inch (1.3 cm) slices and toast them until golden and slightly crunchy, if you like. Put the pesto into a small bowl and stir in the vinegar. Add olive oil as needed to turn the pesto into a smooth sauce that you can drizzle from a spoon.

Arrange the burrata in the center of a dinner plate, and gently tear it open to expose the cream in the center. Pit the fruit as needed and cut it into pieces. Arrange the fruit around the burrata. Drizzle as much pesto sauce as you want over the cheese and fruit, then drizzle on some olive oil and a few thin lashings of honey. Sprinkle sea salt on top and enjoy with extra pesto on the side.

HOMEMADE PESTO

MAKES ABOUT ¾ CUP (180 ML)

1 packed cup (40 g) basil leaves (from 1 large bunch)

1 large garlic clove

¼ cup (25 g) shredded Parmesan

¼ cup (25 g) shredded pecorino Romano, or more Parmesan

1 tablespoon pine nuts, lightly toasted

1 Meyer lemon, for zest and juice

⅓ cup (80 ml) high-quality extra-virgin olive oil

Kosher salt

Put the basil, garlic, Parmesan, pecorino, and pine nuts into a food processor, and use a microplane to grate a little bit of zest from the lemon into the mix. Process everything until you have a relatively smooth paste. Scrape the sides; then, with the processor running, slowly pour the olive oil into the mixture, stopping to scrape the sides as needed. When the sauce has a fairly smooth texture, season it with a squeeze of lemon juice and ¼ teaspoon of salt. Run the processor a few seconds more, then taste and add more lemon juice and salt as needed.

SPANISH TUNA, TOMATO & OLIVE SALAD

1 small heirloom tomato, or 2 to 3 medium vine-ripened tomatoes

Kosher salt

Granulated sugar (optional)

3 to 4 ounces (85 to 115 g) high-quality tuna in olive oil

3 or 4 pitted Castelvetrano olives

Extra-virgin olive oil

Red wine vinegar

Spain is known for amazing ham and great cheese, some glorious stews, lots of out-of-this-world seafood, and all kinds of other treats, but serving fresh vegetables—not so much. I, personally, eat a lot of fresh produce in my regular life, so when I was visiting the Iberian Peninsula a few years ago with my family, I made it a mission to hunt down whatever fresh vegetable dishes I could find. I quickly fell in love with this salad, which mixes rich tinned tuna with bright tomatoes and mild olives. The combination works well even if the tomatoes aren't at their peak, and is hearty enough to make an excellent meal all on its own.

Cut the tomato into irregular pieces about 1 inch (2.5 cm) across, season them with a large pinch of salt, and scatter them onto a plate. (If the tomato is not particularly flavorful, you can add a pinch of sugar.) Drain the tuna and flake it with a fork, then tuck the flakes between the pieces of tomato. Nestle the olives into the salad, drizzle on a little olive oil and about ½ teaspoon of vinegar, and sprinkle on one last pinch of salt. Taste and adjust the seasonings as needed.

Bulk Up the Plate: This salad is nice with some good bread, and a few slices of jamón serrano (or jamón ibérico) would also be good on the side.

TURKISH BREAKFAST FOR DINNER

BREAKFAST SPREAD

2 to 3 ounces (60 to 85 g) feta

Turkish bread, like simit or pide, or similar, such as focaccia

Sliced cucumber

Wedges of tomato

Assorted olives

Clotted cream

Honey

Assorted jams and preserves, such as fig, sour cherry, bitter orange, and/or apricot

MENEMEN

2 eggs

Kosher salt

1 tablespoon unsalted butter

2 teaspoons tomato paste

2 teaspoons Turkish pepper paste

½ small tomato, diced

For a truly well-rounded meal, look no further than a Turkish breakfast. A classic spread includes not just eggs, bread, and jam, but also a variety of cheeses, a bowl of olives, sliced vegetables, and other treats. It offers more variety and flavors than some people get in a full day—all before 9 a.m. The assortment here is based on breakfast spreads from the city of Van and includes menemen, a classic dish of eggs cooked with tomatoes and peppers. Alternate sweet bites with savory or mix and match any way you like.

Arrange the feta, bread, cucumber, tomato, olives, cream, honey, and preserves on plates and in small bowls.

To make the menemen, beat the eggs with a pinch of salt and set them aside. Melt ½ tablespoon of the butter in a small nonstick pan over medium heat, then add the tomato and pepper pastes and toast them, stirring with a rubber spatula, for 1 minute. Add the diced tomato and cook until the pieces start to soften, about 1 minute, then push everything to one side of the pan and turn the heat to low.

Add the remaining ½ tablespoon of butter to the cleared side of the pan and let it melt, then remove the pan from the heat and add the eggs to the melted butter. Scramble the eggs gently, tipping the pan as needed to keep them on one side, separate from the tomato mixture, and putting the pan back on the heat only as much as needed to cook the eggs to soft curds. Stir the tomato mixture into the eggs just as they finish cooking.

BROILED FETA & TOMATOES WITH CRUSTY BREAD

1 cup (165 g) cherry tomatoes

1 sweet mini pepper or part of a slightly spicy pepper, like a Jimmy Nardello or an Italian frying pepper, stemmed and seeded

4 Castelvetrano olives

2 big pinches of fresh oregano leaves

2 tablespoons extra-virgin olive oil

1 teaspoon gochujang

Kosher salt

Freshly ground black pepper

One 4-ounce (115 g) block of feta

½ of a baguette

2 or 3 basil leaves

A couple of years ago, when a viral pasta recipe for broiled feta and tomato pasta started showing up all over the internet, I noticed something strange. The videos started out beautifully, with a square of broiled cheese surrounded by bright, glistening tomatoes, but then cooks dumped pasta into the pan and mixed everything up, ruining the pretty presentation. Instead of following the internet's lead, I stop at that gorgeous in-between step and serve it with crusty bread instead of pasta. I also add some olives for a briny kick, and spice the whole thing with a touch of gochujang. The result is as pretty as it is delicious.

Cut the tomatoes in half lengthwise (or in quarters, if large) and roughly chop the pepper and the olives. Put the vegetables and the oregano in a small baking dish, toss them with the olive oil and gochujang, and season with a big pinch of salt and some pepper. Nestle the feta into the center of the vegetable mix.

Cook everything under the broiler until the tomatoes have split and the top of the cheese is browned (the timing will vary depending on your oven).

Cut the baguette into thin slices and toast them lightly. Chiffonade the basil. When the tomatoes and feta are done, sprinkle the basil on top. To eat, spread some cheese on a piece of baguette and pile on some of the vegetables.

ROTI PIZZA

¼ cup (7 g) cilantro

1 tablespoon mint leaves

1 small garlic clove

½ small jalapeño or serrano chile (optional)

2 teaspoons freshly squeezed lime juice

Kosher salt

Granulated sugar

Ground cumin

Two 7-inch (18 cm) phulka- or chapati-style roti (thawed if frozen)

Extra-virgin olive oil

⅛ small red onion

½ small tomato

½ cup (50 g) shredded Parmesan

If you grew up in the US (or many other Western countries), chances are you used to make some kind of makeshift "pizza" using English muffins or maybe those puffy Boboli breads popular in the 1990s. While those bready snacks were fine for satisfying teenage hunger pangs, fresh or frozen roti are a far better base for making pizza in a pinch. This idea, borrowed from cookbook author Priya Krishna, gives you a thin, crispy "crust" that makes a perfect canvas for a light dusting of flavorful toppings. (Note: If you want, you can use the mint-cilantro chutney from the Mango Chaat Rolls [page 83] instead of the chopped herb-chile mix below.)

Preheat the oven to 400°F (200°C). Roughly chop the cilantro and mint and mince the garlic and the chile, if using. Combine the herbs, garlic, and chile on a chopping board and chop together, using the side of the knife to scoop and fold the edges of the pile to the center occasionally until everything is very finely minced. Transfer the mixture to a small bowl or mortar, season it with the lime juice and a big pinch each of salt, sugar, and cumin, and crush everything with a pestle until you have a very coarse paste.

Put the roti on a baking pan, brush them with a bit of olive oil, and bake them for 4 to 5 minutes, until crisp. While the roti is in the oven, thinly slice the onion and finely chop the tomato. Remove the roti from the oven; divide the cheese, onion, and tomato between them; and put them back in the oven until the cheese is melted, 3 to 5 minutes. Remove the pizzas from the oven, sprinkle some of the herb mixture onto each, and cut them into wedges to eat.

Bulk Up the Plate: For a pizza-parlor experience, pair this with a salad of chopped iceberg lettuce, tomato, and olives with a zingy red wine vinaigrette. Alternatively, lean into the pizzas' Indian flavors with a side of fresh fruit sprinkled with chaat masala.

BALI-IN-CALIFORNIA URAP SALAD WRAPS

DRESSING

1 garlic clove

1 red Fresno chile, seeded and cut into very thin strips

1 makrut lime leaf, spine removed and cut into a chiffonade

¼ cup (30 g) thinly sliced shallot

1½ teaspoons ground coriander

Kosher salt

Freshly ground black pepper

¼ cup (20 g) shredded dried coconut

½ teaspoon ground cumin

¼ teaspoon ground ginger

¼ teaspoon ground turmeric (optional)

1½ teaspoons coconut sugar or brown sugar

3 heaping tablespoons coconut oil

1 tablespoon freshly squeezed lime juice, plus more to taste

This fun, salad-y snack comes from Nora Haron, an Indonesian chef who moved to California more than twenty years ago and is known for reworking her country's classics with fresh, local ingredients. This dish is a perfect example of her approach. It's based on urap, a salad that's usually made with Southeast Asian ingredients like steamed bean sprouts and long beans, but uses California swaps like frisée and Fresno chiles. What holds the whole thing together is the dressing, a mix of dried coconut, spices, coconut oil, and lime juice infused with fresh chile and makrut lime leaf. It gives each bite a bright, complex flavor; I add a little extra here, so you can roll the salad up in cabbage leaves without losing any flavor. (Note: The coconut oil will firm up if it cools, so start with room temperature ingredients.)

To make the dressing, crush the garlic into a paste in a mortar and pestle (or mince it and scrape it into a paste with the side of the knife). Put the garlic, chile, and lime leaf into a metal mixing bowl with the shallot, ½ teaspoon of the coriander, a pinch of salt, and a couple of grinds of pepper; set this aside.

CONTINUED

SALAD

1 packed cup (80 g) thinly sliced cabbage, plus 6 cabbage leaves (from ½ a small head)

1 cup (45 g) frisée cut into 2-inch (5 cm) lengths

¾ cup (70 g) thinly sliced raw green beans (cut at a diagonal, to make long ovals)

4 to 6 basil leaves, thinly sliced

Crispy fried shallots or onions (store-bought) or shrimp chips

Toast the coconut, the remaining 1 teaspoon of coriander, and the cumin, ginger, and turmeric, if using, in a small pot or pan over medium heat, stirring constantly, until it is very fragrant. Add the sugar and continue cooking, scraping the pot constantly to keep the sugar from burning, until the coconut starts to brown, another 1 to 2 minutes. Turn the heat off and add the coconut oil, stirring until it becomes liquid, then pour the mixture over the chile–lime leaf mixture. Add 1 tablespoon of lime juice, mix, and let it sit for 3 to 5 minutes to let the flavors meld.

To make the salad, add the sliced cabbage, frisée, green beans, and basil to the bowl and toss everything together thoroughly (your hands will work better than tongs). If the salad cools and the coconut oil starts to firm up, pop the bowl in a slightly warm oven for a few seconds. Taste the urap and add a little more lime juice if needed. To eat, put a few bites' worth in part of a cabbage leaf, top it with some fried shallots or crumbled shrimp chips, and roll it up into a small wrap.

POLISH-ISH FRESH CHEESE & VEGGIE TOASTS

½ scallion, white and light-green parts only

6 tablespoons (100 g) full-fat, small-curd cottage cheese, such as Good Culture

1 lemon, for zest

Freshly ground pepper

Kosher salt

2 slices German-style pumpernickel or rye bread

½ of an English cucumber

1 French breakfast radish

Fresh dill

Salmon roe (optional)

This snack appeals to both my eastern European side and my hippie roots. Growing up, I didn't love either cottage cheese or the sturdy, nutritionally dense German bread popular in health food stores in the 1980s. But as an adult, I've seen the light. This toast is based on both a popular Polish breakfast dish made with gzik (a mixture of farmer's cheese and minced vegetables) and on Danish smørrebrød (open-faced sandwiches), and it uses both these ingredients to excellent effect. You'll want to use a really dense pumpernickel or rye bread, the kind that often comes packaged in very thinly sliced, compact loaves.

Thinly slice the scallion and mix it with the cottage cheese, ¼ teaspoon of finely grated lemon zest, and a little pepper; taste and add salt if needed. Toast the bread in a toaster oven or in a regular oven set to 400°F (200°C). Cut the cucumber and radish into thin slices, angling the knife to make long oval shapes.

Divide the cottage cheese mixture between the two slices of toast, and smooth it into even layers. Arrange the cucumber and radish slices in overlapping layers, kind of like the scales of a fish, sprinkle with a bit of salt, and top each toast with a few small sprigs of dill, a bit more lemon zest, and a few glistening orbs of salmon roe, if using.

Bulk Up the Plate: Since this dish has both Danish and Polish flavors, it goes well with preserved fish: toast another slice of bread, slather it with salted butter, and pile a few sardines on top.

PANTRY SNACKS

These recipes are the workhorses of any snacking-meal habit. They're always available when you need them, ready to solve your dinner problems when your day goes too long, you're too tired to cook a conventional meal, or you realize an ingredient you were relying on has gone bad (or never made it into your shopping bag). In short, they're lifesavers.

Pantry snacks are, by definition, just that: things you can make with items that keep almost indefinitely in your pantry or fridge—and, in some cases, a fresh ingredient or two that you're likely to have around, like an apple. But just because you don't have to plan ahead for these meals doesn't mean they're boring or second-choice options. In fact, pantry snacks often become our favorite meals, the ones we turn to again and again, not just because they're convenient but because we crave their flavors as much as their ease. Stock your pantry well (see A Snacker's Pantry, page 137), and these recipes will ensure that you never have to panic about dinner, no matter what life throws at you.

FUN PREMADE SNACKS TO ROUND OUT YOUR MEAL

1 50HERTZ TINGLY SICHUAN PEPPER PEANUTS

FOR CRUNCH

What's it like? Salty roasted peanuts with just the right amount of numbing flavor from Sichuan peppers

Try it with: Cold Tofu with Scallions, Tomato & Chile Crisp (page 18)

2 AMANOYA HIMEMARU (JAPANESE RICE CRACKERS)

FOR CRUNCH

What's it like? Sturdy, crunchy rounds of popped rice with a strong sweet-savory flavor and just the right amount of spiciness

Try it with: Salad-y Summer Rolls with a Hawaiian Twist (page 95)

3 ORION TURTLE CHIPS

FOR CRUNCH OR SWEETNESS

What's it like? Multilayered chip-like snack with a soft crunch; available in a variety of flavors, including savory (seaweed, corn, or sour cream and onion), sweet (chocolate churro), and spicy (spicy lime or mala)

Try it with: Kimchi Melt (page 49), Pimento Cheese and Tomato Finger Sandwiches (page 97)

4 GREEN & SUNNY MEE KROB THAI CRISPY RICE NOODLE SNACKS

FOR CRUNCH

What's it like? Wildly flavorful squares of crispy, crunchy thread-like noodles; the Original Sweet & Sour Sauce and Larb Thai Chili Lime flavors are particularly good

Try it with: Salad-y Summer Rolls with a Hawaiian Twist (page 95); Crispy Rice and Chorizo with Herbs and Lettuce (page 112)

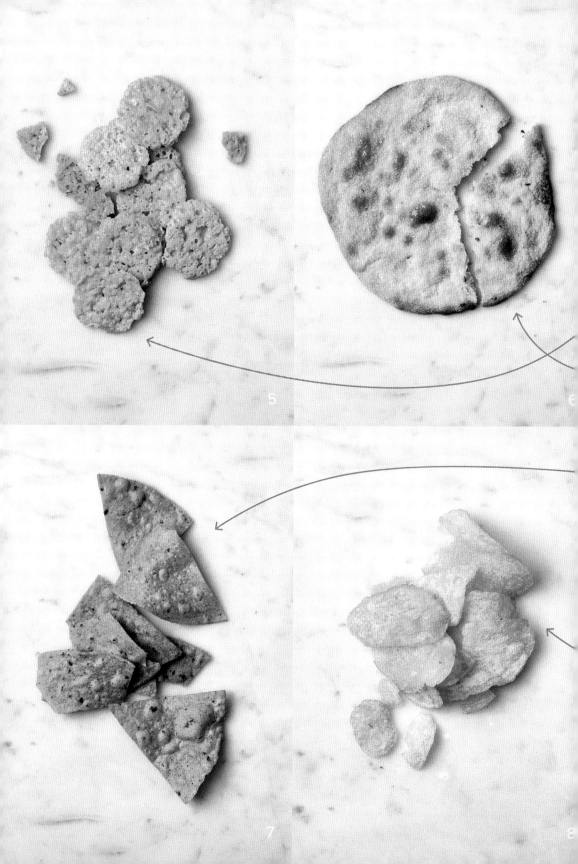

5 PARMCRISPS

FOR CRUNCH

What's it like? Crunchy, umami-rich flavor bombs made from Parmesan cheese

Try it with: Antipasti Board with Roasted Artichoke Hearts (page 66); Classic Bruschetta (page 89); Mix & Match Potato Bites (page 104)

6 INÉS ROSALES OLIVE OIL TORTAS

FOR CRUNCH OR SWEETNESS

What's it like? Round Spanish crackers with a gentle crunch and a range of great flavors including savory (such as rosemary thyme) and sweet (lemon, orange, cinnamon)

Try it with: Crudités with Yogurt-Miso Green Goddess Dip (page 80); assorted cheeses and jams

7 HAVE'A CORN CHIPS

FOR CRUNCH

What's it like? Extra-crispy tortilla chips flavored with a little bit of soy sauce and a hint of lime

Try it with: Deconstructed Guacamole (page 17); Halibut-Avocado Ceviche with Coconut Milk (page 101)

8 TORRES SELECTA POTATO CHIPS

FOR CRUNCH

What's it like? Thin, crisp potato chips made in Spain, in flavors like black truffle, smoked paprika, and Iberian ham

Try it with: Spanish Tuna, Tomato & Olive Salad (page 27)

9 TONGSOOK THAI COCONUT ROLLS

FOR SWEETNESS

What's it like? Delicate, flaky, tuille-like cookies with a light, sweet coconut flavor

Try it with: Crispy Rice & Chorizo with Herbs & Lettuce (page 112); Onigiri with Smoked Salmon (page 98)

10 VIOLET CRUMBLE

FOR SWEETNESS

What's it like? Cubes of airy, crumbly honeycomb candy covered in chocolate

Try it with: Sweet & Spicy Chilled Sesame Noodles (page 115); Caviar Sandwich (page 127)

11 NO BRAND SEASHELL SHAPED SNACK

FOR SWEETNESS

What's it like? Like a slightly denser, crispy-crunchy version of Frosted Flakes cereal (with a hint of sesame), but shaped like tiny seashells

Try it with: Anything! (You'll probably end up eating them all on their own.)

12 NUTELLA & GO!

FOR SWEETNESS

What's it like? Small tubs of Nutella with breadsticks or pretzel sticks for dipping

Try it with: Broiled Feta & Tomatoes with Crusty Bread (page 30); Unstuffed Crab & Avocado (page 128)

SARDINES WITH PICKLED PEPPERS

Tinned sardines (ideally packed in oil)

Olive oil (if needed)

Crunchy, sturdy, whole wheat crackers, such as Ak-Mak

Mild banana pepper rings

Yuzu kosho (optional)

The simplest (and easiest) of all snacking dinners, sardines on crackers has been an obsession in my house for years. It all started when my brilliant friend Beth Kracklauer wrote an article that mentioned that her go-to comfort meal after a hard day is sardines piled on crackers or eaten right out of the tin—with a Manhattan on the side. I immediately made myself the same meal that night using the Ak-Mak crackers I had in my pantry. My then-toddler was super curious about the snack, and as soon as I gave her a bite, she was hooked. Soon "fishies on crackers" was a regular part of our family dinner rotation. Almost a decade later, it's a meal I continue to turn to for both of us when I don't have the time or energy to cook; my daughter gets crudités on the side, I still sometimes opt for a Manhattan or a negroni.

If the sardines weren't packed in olive oil, drain them, add a generous amount of olive oil to the tin, and let the fish absorb some of it. Break some crackers in half crosswise, place a sardine or two on each half, and top each one with a couple of pepper rings and/or a slick of yuzu kosho, if using.

KIMCHI MELT

1 slice white sandwich bread

⅓ cup (60 g) cabbage kimchi

1 tablespoon mayonnaise

¼ teaspoon toasted sesame oil

⅓ cup (30 g) grated medium cheddar

1 small handful classic potato chips

Toasted sesame seeds

This flavorful snack highlights how much our grocery "staples" have changed in the past generation. Even a decade ago, I might not have been able to assume that Westerners of all backgrounds would have access to kimchi; today I'd be shocked if I couldn't find at least one brand in most supermarkets. (If you're not already stashing a jar of cabbage kimchi in the back of your fridge, you're missing out.) In fact, if you need to buy anything for this meal, it might be the sliced white bread, which is no longer the staple it used to be.

Lightly toast the bread. Chop the kimchi and mix it with the mayonnaise and sesame oil in a small bowl. Spread the kimchi mixture onto the toast and top it with half of the cheese, reserving the rest. Cook in a toaster oven or under a broiler until the cheese has just melted (the timing will depend on your oven). Remove the toast from the heat, arrange the potato chips on top, over the melted cheese, and cover them with the remaining cheese. Return the topped toast to the toaster oven or broiler and cook until the cheese has thoroughly melted and the edges of the chips are browned. Sprinkle the toast with a couple big pinches of sesame seeds.

Bulk Up the Plate: This toast goes well with a simple salad of cucumber, carrot, celery, or cabbage dressed in a few drops each of soy sauce and sesame oil, and/or a Bartavelle or Salt & Spice jammy egg (page 71).

WHITE BEAN & SALAMI TOAST

4 salami slices

2 garlic cloves

2 slices sourdough or a long piece of baguette cut in half lengthwise

2 teaspoons extra-virgin olive oil

1½ cups (255 g) drained cooked or canned white beans, such as cannellini

Freshly ground black pepper

Dried oregano

3 tablespoons grated or shredded Parmesan, plus more to garnish

Beans on toast is one of those magical foods that, once assembled, is far more than the sum of its parts. If you've never had it, the combination of these two extremely common (and not super exciting) beige-brown ingredients might sound, well, pretty boring. And yet, the combination works so well that it has become a staple in a variety of countries: in England you'll find a version made of baked beans with sugar and tomato; in Italy you might see white beans flavored with garlic and Parmesan (plus high-quality olive oil, of course).

This version is inspired by the Italian approach, and I've added salami (a staple we keep tucked in the back of the fridge) and a good amount of dried oregano. It's the kind of dish that you might make in a pinch, just because all the ingredients are so easy to keep around, but once you taste it, you'll make it again and again.

Finely chop the salami slices and mince the garlic. Toast the bread. Heat the oil in a small nonstick pan over medium-high heat, then add the salami, garlic, and beans, season everything with a few grinds of pepper (a bit more than you would normally think necessary) and a few generous shakes of oregano. Cook the mixture, stirring, until everything is heated through, about 3 minutes. Turn off the heat and stir in the Parmesan, then pile everything on top of the toasted bread and finish it with more Parmesan.

CONSERVAS WITH PAN CON TOMATE

2 thick slices of rustic white bread, such as pan de cristal or pain au levain, or a long piece of baguette cut in half

1 small garlic clove

½ smallish tomato (cut in half through its equator)

1 tin Spanish conservas, such as sardines, octopus in olive oil, or mussels in escabeche (or 2 tins, for variety)

Spanish olives, such as arbequina (optional)

No style of meal has a snackier vibe than tapas, whether they're served one by one at a bar counter, each with a fresh glass of wine, or as a spread of raciónes shared among friends. While some tapas can be intricate and elaborate, the items in this particular meal—conservas (tinned seafood), a big serving of classic pan con tomate, and maybe a bowl of briny olives—are all foods you probably already have in your kitchen. It's a win for flavor and for convenience.

Lightly toast the bread until it is slightly crisp. Peel the garlic and rub it along one piece of toast. Rub the tomato's cut side onto the same toast until the pulp and seeds have transferred onto the bread; leave the second piece of toast plain.

Open the conservas and set the tin(s), without draining, on a plate; arrange the pan con tomate, the plain slice of toast, and some olives, if using, on another plate. To eat, use a small fork or a toothpick to pile some conservas onto either piece of bread, and use any uneaten bread to sop up the oil or sauce in the tin.

Bulk Up the Plate: For a larger meal, stop by a Spanish market for two other tapa classics: jamón serrano (or jamón ibérico) and manchego cheese.

GROWN-UP "PB&J" RICE CRACKERS

½ cup (70 to 80 g) assorted dried fruit, such as apricots, dates, cranberries, raisins, and coconut flakes

½ apple

½ teaspoon honey, plus more as needed

1 lemon wedge (optional)

4 extra-thin rice cakes (such as Lundberg Thin Stackers)

Nut butter(s)

Flaky sea salt

If you haven't had one in a while, a good peanut butter and jelly sandwich is a revelation. The creamy savoriness of the nut butter, the sunny sweetness of the jelly—we might think of this as kid food, but there's a reason our little ones love it so much. This snack pairs that iconic flavor combo with another childhood favorite—crispy, crunchy rice cakes—and makes it a little more grown-up by swapping the sugary jelly for a mix of fresh and dried fruits. You can play with the combination any way you want, trying different mixes of dried fruits and using whatever kind of nut butter(s) you enjoy.

Pile the dried fruit on a cutting board and finely chop it all together, using the side of the knife to scoop and fold the edges of the pile to the center so that the different fruits mix together. Finely chop enough of the apple that you have about half as much apple as dried fruit by volume, then add it to the dried fruit and chop and scoop everything together until well mixed. Transfer to a small bowl and mix in the honey and a small squeeze of lemon juice, if you like.

Spread a thin layer of nut butter on each of the rice cakes (or different nut butters on each rice cake), top each with a quarter of the fruit mixture, and sprinkle everything with a bit of salt. If your fruit mixture is more sour than sweet, drizzle a little more honey on top.

SPICED POPCORN THREE WAYS

POPCORN BASE

¼ cup (55 g) popcorn kernels

2 tablespoons vegetable oil

A bowl of popcorn (with or without a big glass of wine) is perhaps the most classic snacking dinner, perfect for a night when you get home late or are just tired and need to shut out the world with a good movie binge. I've always turned to a simple mix of nutritional yeast and butter for my toppings ("brewer's yeast" was popular in my hippie-filled hometown), but when my friend Karen Shimizu made me a bowl seasoned with pepper and spices, I realized what a great blank canvas these fluffy white kernels can be. Here are three of my new-favorite popcorn flavorings: (1) a mix of furikake and garlic powder with lemon and sesame that reminds me of the flavors in a classic fish house special, (2) a spice blend that uses the flavors found in Chinese shao kao barbecue (the skewers you eat at roadside stands in northern China), and (3) a variation that takes its cue from truffle fries. Make just one or try all three at once! (I usually make these with loose popping corn, but unseasoned microwave popcorn would also work.)

To make the popcorn, put the kernels and oil into a medium pot and heat on medium, covered. When the kernels begin to pop, start shaking the pan occasionally and tipping it from side to side to sift the unpopped kernels to the bottom. When the popping has slowed so there are 3 or 4 seconds between pops, remove the pot from the heat and shake it vigorously to allow any last corn to pop; set it aside, still covered.

CONTINUED

GARLICKY FURIKAKE TOPPING

3 tablespoons unsalted butter

1 tablespoon nori- and sesame-based furikake or furikake with katsuobushi

1 teaspoon garlic powder

½ teaspoon freshly squeezed lemon juice

¼ teaspoon toasted sesame oil

SHAO KAO TOPPING

3 tablespoons unsalted butter

¾ teaspoon Korean chile powder

½ teaspoon ground cumin

½ teaspoon garlic powder

¼ teaspoon toasted sesame oil

Pinch of kosher salt

Pinch of granulated sugar

TRUFFLE-PARMESAN TOPPING

2 tablespoons butter

1 tablespoon truffle oil (made from real truffle)

Kosher salt

A chunk of Parmesan

For the **furikake** or **shao kao** topping, melt the butter on the stove or in the microwave (take care not to let it bubble over), then stir in the rest of the topping ingredients. Put half the popcorn into a medium bowl and drizzle it with half the topping, spreading it out as much as possible, then add the remaining popcorn and drizzle on the rest of the topping. Use your hands to mix everything together and spread out the seasonings.

For the **truffle-Parmesan** topping, melt the butter on the stove or in the microwave (take care not to let it bubble over), then stir in the truffle oil. Put half the popcorn into a medium bowl, drizzle it with half the butter, spreading it out as much as possible, sprinkle in a big pinch of salt, and use a microplane zester to grate a really generous flurry of Parmesan on top. Add the remaining popcorn, butter, salt, and another generous flurry of Parmesan, and use your hands to mix everything together and spread out the seasonings.

FORIANA & PARMESAN TOASTS

2 pieces whole wheat bread

1 large garlic clove

2 tablespoons walnut pieces

2 tablespoons pine nuts

2 tablespoons golden raisins

1 teaspoon dried oregano

2 tablespoons extra-virgin olive oil

¼ cup (25 g) shredded Parmesan

Kosher salt

The first time I had pasta with foriana sauce—a mix of nuts, raisins, garlic, and herbs—it totally blew my mind. The jumble of ingredients didn't look particularly interesting, but the blend of sweet, savory, and aromatic flavors was irresistible. That flavor, plus the fact that foriana is made of shelf-stable ingredients that I already kept in my pantry, quickly made this food a beloved staple. Here I've created an even simpler, snackified version of this fantastic meal by piling the mixture on top of whole wheat toast. I've also stirred in some shredded Parmesan (the kind that comes in tubs), which melts in the toaster oven and helps hold the other ingredients together.

Lightly toast the bread. While it's toasting, combine the garlic, walnuts, pine nuts, raisins, and oregano on a chopping board and finely chop everything together, occasionally using the side of the knife to scoop and fold the edges of the pile to the center. Transfer the foriana mixture to a small bowl and stir in the olive oil, the Parmesan, and a pinch of salt. When the toast is ready, divide the foriana between the pieces and spread it out in an even layer. Cook the toasts in a toaster oven or under a broiler just until the Parmesan melts and the top edges of the nuts are starting to turn brown (the timing will vary depending on your oven).

BLACK BEAN PICADILLO WITH CHIPS

2 tablespoons raisins

¾ cup (165 g) drained canned diced tomatoes

5 pitted green olives

1 large garlic clove

1 tablespoon extra-virgin olive oil

1 cup (165 g) drained cooked or canned black beans

¼ teaspoon kosher salt

¼ teaspoon Japanese soy sauce (such as Kikkoman)

⅛ teaspoon ground cinnamon

⅛ teaspoon smoked paprika

Tortilla chips

Classic Cuban picadillo—ground meat flavored with sweet raisins, savory tomatoes, salty olives, and fragrant cinnamon—is the ultimate comfort food. Here, I've turned those same flavors into an easy-to-make warm dip that uses black beans in place of the meat (with a hint of soy sauce to add some umami). The result can be eaten warm or cold with tortilla chips.

Roughly chop the raisins and put them into a small bowl with a little warm water to soften for 5 minutes. Roughly chop the tomatoes (to cut the chunks into smaller pieces) and set them aside. Thinly slice the olives and mince the garlic.

Heat the olive oil in a small nonstick pan over high heat. Drain the raisins and add them and the olives to the pan. Cook, stirring a bit, until some pieces are starting to brown, about 2 minutes. Add the tomato and garlic and cook, stirring frequently, until the tomato has lost some of its volume and looks a little bit cooked, 3 to 4 minutes. Add the beans, season them with the salt and soy sauce, turn the heat to low, and cook until they're just warmed, another minute or two. Add the cinnamon and paprika and cook for 30 seconds, stirring, to toast the spices, then transfer the bean mixture to a bowl. Eat the beans warm or at room temperature, with the chips.

OKONOMIYAKI TATER TOTS

10 ounces (280 g) frozen tater tots

1 scallion, white and light-green parts only

Okonomiyaki sauce

Kewpie mayonnaise

Nori- and sesame seed-based furikake

1 handful katsuobushi

Okonomiyaki, the Japanese cabbage pancake, always brings back memories of late-night meals at street stalls in Tokyo. This recipe uses the same flavors as okonomiyaki, but instead of cabbage, I use oven-baked tater tots as my base—their centers are tender enough to be reminiscent of the original, but their outsides are lovely and crunchy. Then I pile on all my favorite okonomiyaki toppings: sweet-savory sauce, mayonnaise, furikake, fresh scallion, and katsuobushi (thinly shaved bonito flakes). The result is fast and easy enough to make any night of the week.

Cook the tater tots in an oven according to the instructions on the package. While they're roasting, cut the scallion in half lengthwise and then cut it very thinly crosswise. When the tater tots are ready, arrange them in a single layer on a plate, snuggled close together, and make thin zigzags of the okonomiyaki sauce and mayonnaise over them. Sprinkle on the scallion and a generous amount of the furikake. Lastly, distribute the katsuobushi on top of everything; the shavings will "dance" as the heat from the tater tots moves them.

Bulk Up the Plate: If you want a really hearty meal, put a fried egg on top of the dish. For something lighter, dress celery sticks in some sesame oil, a little soy sauce, and a good shake of furikake to make a salad similar to the one served at Bar Goto in New York.

MAKE-YOUR-OWN SPICY TUNA HAND ROLLS

½ cup (100 g) Japanese short-grain rice

½ teaspoon seasoned rice vinegar, or regular rice vinegar mixed with a pinch each of salt and sugar

1 Persian cucumber or a 4-inch (10 cm) length of English cucumber

Kosher salt

1 mini 3-ounce (85 g) can tuna, drained

1 tablespoon mayonnaise

2½ teaspoons sriracha

⅛ teaspoon toasted sesame oil

3 sheets toasted nori

Toasted sesame seeds

On nights when I want the kind of meal where I get to play with ingredients and customize with each bite, I arrange a plate full of everything I need to make sushi hand rolls. The fillings vary depending on what I'm in the mood for, but the one combo I turn to again and again is a spicy tuna salad with a side of wilted cucumber. When spicy tuna rolls were first invented (in Seattle, in the 1980s), the mix was made of raw tuna. But the at-home-friendly version with canned tuna is also delicious—and a whole lot simpler.

Rinse the rice well, until the water runs clear, and drain it. Put the rice in a rice cooker or a medium pot with ½ cup (120 ml) of water. If using a pot, bring the water just to a boil over medium heat, then give the rice a stir to make sure none is sticking to the bottom. Cover the pot and turn the heat to low. Simmer the rice for 12 minutes, then turn the heat off and let the rice sit undisturbed so that it continues to steam in its own heat for another 10 minutes. When the rice is ready, drizzle the vinegar over it and mix well.

While the rice is cooking, prepare the fillings: Slice the cucumber into thin rounds or strips (or both), massage it with two big pinches of salt, and set it aside in a small bowl to wilt. Flake the tuna and mix it with the mayonnaise, sriracha, and sesame oil in another small bowl. Cut the sheets of nori into halves or quarters. Lay out all the elements—rice, cucumber, tuna, nori, and sesame seeds—separately so you can create your own hand rolls.

ANTIPASTI BOARD WITH ROASTED ARTICHOKE HEARTS

One 6-ounce (170 g) jar quartered artichoke hearts in brine

4 teaspoons extra-virgin olive oil

¼ to ½ teaspoon gochujang

3 tablespoons julienned sun-dried tomatoes in oil

Thinly sliced mortadella

Pizza bianca or focaccia

Mild pickled green peppers

Parmesan in big chunks

Olives

While a plate of antipasti is usually served before lunch or dinner (the name literally means "before meal"), the classic Italian combination of cheeses, meats, and marinated vegetables has everything you need for an absolutely perfect snacking dinner all on its own.

I like to balance these classic flavors with something sweet (like roasted sun-dried tomatoes) and something tangy and spicy (like pickled peppers), plus a few hunks of cheese and some mortadella (presliced at the deli counter). But the real stars on my plate are roasted artichoke hearts. I cook them using a technique borrowed from my friend Helen Rosner and add my own twist with a little bit of gochujang for a hit of sweet-savory heat.

Preheat the oven to 450°F (230°C). While it's heating, drain the artichoke hearts, pressing them to remove as much liquid as possible, then mix them with the olive oil and gochujang in a small bowl, massaging in the gochujang if necessary to make sure it's distributed well. Spread the artichoke pieces on a small sheet pan and roast for 20 minutes, flipping them halfway through. Put the sun-dried tomato pieces on the sheet pan in big clumps, and continue to roast everything until the tomatoes are sizzling and have started to darken at the edges, 2 or 3 minutes. Arrange the roasted vegetables, mortadella, pizza bianca, peppers, cheese, and olives on a cheese board or tray.

CLASSIC SNACKS

&VARIATIONS

These are the foods that likely come to mind when you hear the word "snacks"—the cheese-and-cracker plates or onigiri you ate after school as a kid, the street-food treats you've nibbled on while walking through a market, the dips you scoop up at parties, the noodles you slurp down at midnight. These recipes come from a variety of snacking traditions all across the world and they're all based on tried-and-true favorites.

That said, most of these recipes up the ante a bit, taking a classic to a new place by adding flavors or elements that make your meal extra fun (or bulk it up so it's dinner-worthy). Others have been simplified so they're easier to make in a home kitchen with minimum effort. A few just leave the flavors in their most recognizable form. All of them should trigger lots of snacking memories—or give you a peek into someone else's.

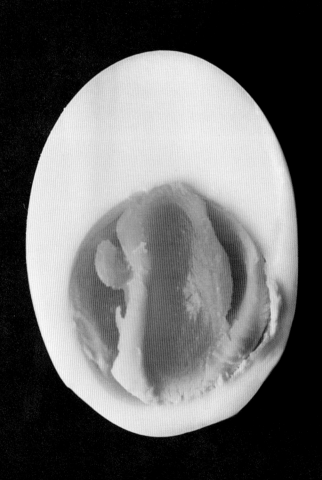

JAMMY EGGS

A good jammy egg—the kind that walks the line between a runny yolk and a fully hard-boiled egg—makes a perfect addition to any snacking meal. You can eat them on their own or add any number of delicious toppings (I've shared my favorites on the next spread). The key to these eggs is their texture: centers should be firm enough to hold together but still be soft and velvety, right between liquid and solid.

The time it takes your eggs to cook will depend entirely on their size and how cold they are to start with (this recipe assumes large, refrigerated eggs). To avoid runny, undercooked eggs, start out by testing just one; if after 8 minutes the center is still runny instead of just a bit gooey, add another minute to the cook time and test again.

8-MINUTE EGGS

Heat 4 to 5 inches (10 to 13 cm) of water in a medium pot until it boils, then use a slotted spoon to carefully lower anywhere from one to four eggs into the water, making sure they're fully submerged. When the water comes back to a gentle boil, set a timer for 8 minutes. While the eggs cook, combine ice cubes and cold tap water in a bowl to make an ice bath. When the eggs are done, use the slotted spoon to transfer them to the ice bath; let them cool for at least 5 minutes. Carefully peel the eggs, cut them in half lengthwise, and add toppings (see next page).

CONTINUED

1 SATURDAY BAGEL

Top it with: Everything spice (mix garlic powder, onion powder, poppy seeds, sesame seeds, and kosher salt)

Try it with: Deconstructed Winter Fruit Fattoush (page 117); Sweet Potato Chip "Salad" with Hot Honey & Fresh Herbs (page 21)

2 THE BARTAVELLE

Top it with: Small dollop of Kewpie mayonnaise and a high-quality anchovy filet

Try it with: Antipasti Board with Roasted Artichoke Hearts (page 66); Kimchi Melt (page 49); Corn & Spinach Tofu Banchan (page 122)

3 GREEN EGGS & HAM

Top it with: Prosciutto and pesto

Try it with: Pimento Cheese & Tomato Finger Sandwiches (page 97); Classic Bruschetta (page 89)

4 NOT-QUITE DEVILED

Top it with: Small dollops of mayo and Dijon mustard plus a pinch of minced pickle

Try it with: Pimento Cheese & Tomato Finger Sandwiches (page 97); Caviar Sandwich (page 127)

5 INSTANT SAMBAL TELUR

Top it with: Jarred sambal and fresh basil leaf

Try it with: Crispy Rice & Chorizo with Herbs & Lettuce (page 112); Bali-in-California Urap Salad Wraps (page 34)

6 SALT & SPICE

Top it with: Aleppo pepper and flaky salt

Try it with: Everything (you can't go wrong with this combo)

7 À LA PROVENÇALE

Top it with: Minced sun-dried tomatoes, green olives, and a pinch of salt

Try it with: Crudités with Yogurt-Miso Green Goddess Dip (page 80)

8 SHORTCUT BANCHAN

Top it with: Chopped kimchi, thinly sliced scallion, and sesame seeds

Try it with: Corn & Spinach Tofu Banchan (page 122); Onigiri with Smoked Salmon (page 98)

9 SICHUAN ZINGER

Top it with: Chile crisp, Sichuan pepper oil, sesame seeds, and thinly sliced scallion

Try it with: Cold Tofu with Scallions, Tomato & Chile Crisp (page 18); Classic Bruschetta (page 89)

APPLE SLICES & CHEDDAR WITH CRACKERS & JAM

¼ small fennel bulb

Kosher salt

Medium-sharp cheddar cheese

1 medium sweet-tart apple, such as Envy or Fuji

Flavorful whole wheat crackers, such as Back to Nature crispy wheat or Carr's whole wheat crackers

Orange marmalade

Brie with a baguette might be sophisticated, and mozzarella with tomatoes may make a perfect summer bite, but for sheer nostalgic happiness, nothing beats cheddar on apple slices. This simple combination is sweet and salty, light and rich all at once—and brings back memories of sitting with my siblings at the kitchen table after a day at kindergarten. Now that I'm older, I up the flavor ante by adding some sweet-bitter orange marmalade to my plate along with some thin slices of fragrant fennel; both work perfectly on top of the cheese (separately or together). To bulk up the meal, so it's hearty enough for dinner, I add whole wheat crackers, another classic vehicle for the cheese and toppings.

Thinly slice the fennel and rub the slices with a couple of big pinches of salt, then set them aside to soften for a few minutes. Cut the cheese into thin, square pieces and slice the apple. Drain away any liquid the salted fennel has released, and arrange everything on a plate with some crackers and a little bowl of the marmalade. Enjoy the cheese, crackers, apples, fennel, and jam in a variety of combinations.

LOADED INSTANT RAMEN WITH TOMATO & HERBS

1 packet of ramen, preferably a standard flavor like shio, miso, tonkotsu, or spicy

1 medium tomato

1 large handful cilantro, leaves and thin stems only

5 basil leaves

1 scallion, white and light-green parts only

Vegetable oil

1 egg

Chile crisp (optional)

In the West, instant ramen is usually considered a college dorm-room snack, something quick and cheap students can use to fuel late-night study sessions. In Japan and other parts of East Asia, however, instant ramen is a convenient way to make a bowl of noodles with pretty much all the toppings you'd find on regular ramen—people add everything from chashu pork belly to fish cakes. Here, I've split the difference: I skip the more time-consuming toppings while still adding lots of flavor with fresh herbs and tomato, a combination reminiscent of noodles I fell for when I lived in southwestern China. I also take an extra minute to fry an egg to put on top—a quick alternative to a traditional ramen egg. (Note: If you buy a package of ramen without English instructions, don't stress; the kanji for "minute" is 分, so look for that character and you'll know that "3分" over a picture of boiling noodles means "boil for 3 minutes.")

Bring water to a boil in a medium pot (using as much water as specified on the ramen package). Meanwhile, dice the tomato, roughly chop the cilantro and the basil, and thinly slice the scallion. When the water boils, cook the noodles (and their seasonings) according to the package instructions, adding the tomato to the pot 1 minute before the noodles are done. Transfer the soup to a large bowl and stir in the herbs.

While the soup cools slightly, heat a slick of oil in a nonstick pan and fry the egg until the edges are starting to brown and crisp; slide it into the ramen bowl. Drizzle in some chile crisp, if using.

SWEET-SPICY-NUMBING QUESO

4 ounces (115 g) Velveeta

2 tablespoons whole milk

Kosher salt

3 tablespoons finely chopped mango

1 teaspoon chile crisp, plus more to taste

¼ to ½ teaspoon Sichuan pepper oil (from red Sichuan peppers), plus more to taste

Tortilla chips

The first time I tried queso, I could practically feel the summer sun—even though I was in a cramped NYC apartment in the dead of winter. So when I recently decided to make queso for myself, I opted to skip the traditional add-ins and use flavors from one of *my* favorite warm places: the subtropical part of Yunnan, a province in southwestern China where I used to live and work. This combination of cheese with sweet mango, spicy chile crisp, and numbing Sichuan peppercorn oil might not be traditional, but the flavors are weirdly wonderful together. (Note: You can also make this dish with jarred queso—regular or vegan—instead of melting Velveeta and milk together.)

Roughly chop the cheese and put it in a heatproof bowl with the milk, then microwave the mixture, stirring occasionally, until the cheese has fully melted. Add a big pinch of salt and whisk the mixture until it has a uniform texture. Pile the mango in the center of the bowl, and drizzle the chile crisp and pepper oil over everything. Eat while hot with the tortilla chips, adding more chile crisp or pepper oil to taste.

Bulk Up the Plate: To add something fresh to your meal (and stay with the Tex-Mex-meets-southwestern-China vibe), sprinkle salt, ground chile, and lime juice on some fruit, cucumber, and jicama; alternatively, just make a big pile of crudités to munch on in between bites of queso.

CRUDITÉS WITH YOGURT-MISO GREEN GODDESS DIP

1 small garlic clove

1 anchovy packed in olive oil (optional)

½ cup (15 g) flat-leaf parsley, leaves and thin stems only

¼ cup (10 g) roughly chopped chives

2 tablespoons tarragon leaves

1 cup (240 g) whole-fat Greek yogurt

1 tablespoon white miso, plus more to taste

2 teaspoons freshly squeezed lemon juice, plus more to taste

Kosher salt

Freshly ground black pepper

Assorted vegetables such as tender celery stalks, carrot sticks, French breakfast radishes, snap peas, endive leaves, radicchio leaves

Vibrant, zesty green goddess dressing is a California classic, invented at the Palace Hotel in San Francisco in 1923. My version turns the dressing into a dip by swapping out the usual mayonnaise and sour cream for thick Greek yogurt so that you can scoop up all the flavor with sliced vegetables. I also add a big spoonful of white miso paste, which adds a wonderful hit of sweet umami (and some healthy probiotic bacteria). The result is a bright, vibrant treat that also happens to be really healthy. (Note: This recipe makes enough dip for two meals; if you have a mini food processor that will pulverize a smaller volume of ingredients, feel free to cut the amounts in half to make a single serving.)

Put the garlic, anchovy (if using), parsley, chives, and tarragon into a food processor and pulse until everything is finely chopped. Add the yogurt, miso, and lemon juice and process, scraping the sides as necessary, until the mixture becomes a smooth sauce. Season with a pinch of salt and a couple grinds of pepper; taste, and add a bit more miso or lemon juice if needed. Enjoy as a dip for the vegetables.

Bulk Up the Plate: Pair this with a Salt & Spice or À la Provençale jammy egg (page 71), or spread some of the dip on a piece of baguette. Mild black olives—the kind you might have put on your fingers as a kid—also go well here.

MANGO CHAAT ROLLS

1 large mango,
or 2 or 3 small ones

2 tablespoons finely
chopped shallot or
red onion

2 teaspoons Mint-
Cilantro Chutney
(recipe follows, or
store-bought)

½ teaspoon minced
serrano chile

1 teaspoon finely
grated lime zest

2 teaspoons freshly
squeezed lime juice,
plus more to taste

½ teaspoon chaat
masala, plus more
for garnish

Ghee or butter

2 hot dog buns

Tamarind chutney
(store bought;
optional)

1 tablespoon sev

1 tablespoon boondi

Cilantro

Mint leaves

Kosher salt

South Asian snacks form a whole culinary universe all by themselves. Chaat—the many varieties of sweet-savory-spicy snacks that range from fried potato-chickpea patties to chopped-up samosas to crispy mixes of fried crunchies, all dressed generously with spices and chutneys—practically fuel the daily life of sprawling cities across Bangladesh, Pakistan, India, and other subcontinent countries. This one comes from Pervaiz Shallwani, the award-winning journalist and chef behind the New York-based pop-up Chaat Dog. His menus include a variety of fruit chaats to serve on hot dogs, and mango is a crowd favorite. Here, I pile it into a bun, leaving out the dog so the chaat stands on its own. Two chutneys, a good sprinkling of boondi and sev (crispy, crunchy toppings used in many chaats), and fresh herbs round out the flavors.

Peel the mango and cut it into smallish pieces (you should have about 1¼ cups / 190 g). Combine the shallot, chutney, serrano, lime zest, 2 teaspoons lime juice, and the chaat masala in a mixing bowl; fold in the mango. Adjust the seasonings and lime juice to taste.

Heat a little ghee in a pan and toast both sides of the hot dog buns. Pile the mango chaat into the buns, drizzle on some tamarind chutney, if using, and sprinkle on the sev and boondi. Roughly chop the cilantro and mint and sprinkle it on everything, along with some salt and more chaat masala, to taste.

Bulk Up the Plate: For a heartier meal, follow Pervaiz's lead and use this mixture as he originally intended it: on a hot dog.

MINT-CILANTRO CHUTNEY

MAKES ½ CUP (100 G)

1 small garlic clove

½ small serrano chile

Juice of ½ lime, plus more as needed

1½ teaspoons apple cider vinegar, plus more as needed

1½ teaspoons extra-virgin olive oil, plus more as needed

Kosher salt

3 cups (90 g) roughly chopped cilantro leaves and stems

1 cup (15 g) lightly packed mint leaves

Combine the garlic, chile, lime juice, vinegar, olive oil, and a pinch of salt in a food processor and blend until combined. Scrape down the sides, add the cilantro and mint, and blend the mixture until smooth, adding a bit more lime juice and olive oil as needed to form a paste. Adjust the salt, lime, and vinegar to taste. The chutney can be refrigerated in an airtight container for up to a week.

CHORIZO & BLACK BEAN NACHOS

3½ ounces (100 g) sturdy tortilla chips

1½ cups (140 g) grated cheddar or Jack cheese

1 ounce (30 g) thinly sliced, Spanish-style (cured) chorizo

¾ cup (155 g) drained canned or cooked black beans

¼ cup (45 g) diced fresh tomato

Sour cream

Diced avocado

Cilantro leaves and thin stems, roughly chopped

For many eaters, nachos made the leap from the snack menu to the dinner menu a long time ago, but I still consider them a snack—and, therefore, the perfect snacking dinner. They're easy to throw together and can be made with pretty much any ingredients and flavors you crave. In fact, the key to taking nachos from a ballpark or movie theater version to a proper dinner is to add a variety of filling toppings. This version uses ingredients that I pretty much always have on hand and that don't require any cooking. All I have to do is chop them up, pile them on tortilla chips with a bunch of cheese, and throw them in the toaster oven or slide them under the broiler.

Spread the chips out on a quarter-sheet pan (or on one side of a half-sheet pan), making an even layer so you can't see much of the pan between the chips. Sprinkle about a third of the cheese evenly over the chips. Cut the chorizo slices into thin strips, then cut them crossway into small pieces, so you have chorizo confetti. Warm the beans. Distribute the beans, chorizo, and tomato evenly over the chips (tucking some in between overlapping spots), then top everything with the remaining cheese. Broil the nachos until the cheese is melted and some of it is bubbling (the timing will depend on your oven). Slide the nachos onto a large plate and top with sour cream, avocado, and cilantro.

MAKESHIFT JIANBING

2 eggs

½ scallion, white and light-green parts

Tian mian jiang (Chinese sweet bean sauce, also sold as "sauce for Peking duck")

One 8-inch (20 cm) frozen youtiao (Chinese "crullers" or "fried sticks"; optional)

2 frozen plain dosas, thawed, or flour tortillas

Sesame seeds

Douban jiang (Chinese chili bean sauce, often labeled "toban djan")

Hot and tender, sweet and spicy, jianbing is my idea of a perfect snack. This Chinese street food is particularly popular as a morning treat—I used to grab one from a street cart in Beijing's hutongs (little alleyways) as a late breakfast—but it's great at any time of day. Jianbing are traditionally made on a big, flat griddle similar to the kind French vendors use for crepes, and they have a very thin pancake-like base. But you can make a smaller, faster version at home by using a premade dosa or a wheat tortilla.

Vendors in China put a variety of fillings in their jianbing depending on what part of the country they're in, and while youtiao (a Chinese fried cruller) is the most classic filling, I've seen everything from shredded potato to lettuce and hot dogs. This version is an ode to the simple ones I first fell for, and includes just a couple of sauces (one sweet, one spicy), sliced scallions, sesame seeds, and the option to add youtiao (which you can find frozen at Chinese supermarkets)—though I often make it without any filling other than the flavorful sauces. While jianbing are traditionally quite large, this recipe makes two smaller ones that, together, are a single serving.

Break the eggs into a small bowl and lightly beat them. Thinly slice the scallion. Measure out 2 teaspoons of sweet bean sauce and mix in ½ teaspoon of water, to thin it. Reheat the youtiao (if using) according to the package instructions, then cut it into thick slices.

CONTINUED

Heat a medium nonstick pan and toast a dosa on one side for about 1 minute, until warmed and lightly golden. Flip the dosa, then pour half the beaten egg over it and use a spatula to spread the egg out in an even layer so that it just barely spills over the edges. Sprinkle half the scallion evenly over the egg and shake on some sesame seeds.

When the egg is set around the edges, flip the dosa over so that the egg is directly on the pan. Turn the heat to low and brush the surface of the dosa with a thin layer of the chile sauce and the thinned sweet bean sauce. If using the youtiao, arrange half the slices in a line down the center of the pancake, overlapping them like fallen dominos if needed so they all fit; fold the sides of the pancake over the youtiao. If not using youtiao, just fold the pancake into quarters and remove it from the pan. Repeat the process with the remaining ingredients to make a second jianbing.

CLASSIC BRUSCHETTA

2 small-to-medium vine-ripened tomatoes

1 medium garlic clove

4 to 6 basil leaves

½ teaspoon kosher salt

Granulated sugar, if needed

2 teaspoons extra-virgin olive oil, plus more for the toasts

⅓ of a soft baguette

While not exactly revelatory or surprising, tomato bruschetta is one of the world's most perfect snacking foods. The simple combination of tomato and basil on toast with some olive oil and salt is, somehow, almost magically ideal. It's fresh and flavorful and light and hearty all at the same time. Once you have one piece, you'll want to eat the entire tray—which is exactly what I recommend here. I like my bruschetta with a bit of bite from fresh garlic, so I've included that in this recipe. I also add a pinch of sugar to my tomatoes, when needed (read: anytime I can't get perfectly ripe, flavorful summer fruits) to bump up their flavor.

Finely chop the tomatoes, removing and discarding the fibrous areas below the stems. Mince the garlic and chiffonade the basil. Mix these ingredients together in a small bowl with the salt, then taste; if your tomatoes are bland, add a pinch of sugar. Stir in the olive oil and let the mixture sit and meld.

Cut the baguette into slices about ¾-inch (2 cm) thick (don't use the end piece). Toast the slices until lightly golden, then brush them with olive oil. Spoon the tomato mixture onto the toasts, leaving some of the tomato water in the bowl so the bread doesn't get soggy.

Bulk Up the Plate: To add protein to this meal, enjoy it with some slices of prosciutto or a Green Eggs & Ham or Sichuan Zinger jammy egg (page 71).

ESQUITES WITH CHIPS

2 ears sweet yellow corn, shucked

½ small scallion, white and light-green parts only

6 tablespoons (100 g) Kewpie mayonnaise

3 tablespoons grated cotija cheese, plus more to garnish

¾ teaspoon grated lime zest

1 teaspoon freshly squeezed lime juice, plus a lime wedge, to serve

1 teaspoon ancho chile powder, plus more to garnish

Kosher salt

Freshly ground black pepper

Cilantro

Tortilla chips

Sweet summer corn is basically a perfect food all on its own, but to really make a meal of it, you'll want to add some fat and acid and heat—that is, you might want to turn it into the classic Mexican street food esquites. This version of the dish comes from Matthew Meyer, the co-owner of the bar and restaurant Low Bar in Oakland, California, which focuses on Chicano flavors. Matt first fell in love with this snack when he was a kid in San Diego; he and his mom went to Tijuana regularly to shop and see family, and along the way they'd find a street vendor and pick up a cup of this hearty treat.

Roast the corn under the broiler, turning with tongs as necessary, until it is cooked through and lightly charred in some places (the timing will vary depending on your oven). Let the corn cool enough that you can hold onto it comfortably, then hold it upright in a medium-sized mixing bowl and cut the kernels off into the bowl with a kitchen knife. Thinly slice the scallion and add it to the corn along with the mayonnaise, cheese, lime zest and juice, and chile powder, and season with salt and pepper. Mix everything well, taste, and adjust the seasonings. Top the esquites with a little more cotija, a pinch of ancho chile powder, and some cilantro, and squeeze on some lime. To eat, scoop up big bites with the tortilla chips.

SHRIMP COCKTAIL WITH CITRUS-GOCHUJANG SEAFOOD SAUCE

POACHED SHRIMP

12 jumbo (size 21 / 25) peeled, deveined shrimp, fresh or thawed (about ½ pound / 225 g)

2 garlic cloves

½ bay leaf

½ lemon

1 teaspoon kosher salt

COCKTAIL SAUCE

¼ cup (70 g) ketchup

1 tablespoon prepared horseradish

1 teaspoon gochujang

1 teaspoon freshly squeezed lemon juice

¼ teaspoon freshly squeezed orange or tangerine juice

⅛ teaspoon garlic powder

Worcestershire sauce

Kosher salt

Freshly ground pepper

The first time I was served shrimp cocktail, I almost couldn't believe my eyes. I was about eight years old, sitting in an elegant restaurant with a Very Special Adult (my godfather, the documentarian Mel Lawrence), when a waiter placed a towering goblet of pink and red in front of me. The cup was sitting on a paper doily, and the shrimp were curled elegantly around the rim.

Thanks to this memory, shrimp cocktail still feels like an elegant dish to me, even though it turns out it's actually easy to make. These days, I poach the shrimp myself and make cocktail sauce from scratch so that I can add a bit of gochujang, for a bit of funky heat, and a squeeze of orange juice for a touch of sweetness.

Put the shrimp into a medium pot with the garlic, bay leaf, lemon half, and salt. Add enough water to cover the shrimp by 1 inch (2.5 cm), then cook, uncovered, over high heat until the shrimp are just cooked through and opaque at their thickest spots. (If you want to be really precise about it, use a cooking thermometer to test the water and drain the shrimp when the water reaches 170°F / 77°C.) Drain the shrimp in a colander and run cold water over them for a minute to stop the cooking, then let them chill in the refrigerator while you make the cocktail sauce.

Combine the ketchup, horseradish, gochujang, lemon juice, orange juice, and garlic powder in a small bowl. Season with a dash of Worcestershire sauce, a pinch of salt, and a grind of fresh pepper, and stir everything well.

Bulk Up the Plate: If you want to add something fresh and crunchy, turn to foods you can dunk in the cocktail sauce, like celery ribs, small carrots, mild radishes.

SALAD-Y SUMMER ROLLS WITH A HAWAIIAN TWIST

SUMMER ROLLS

½ carrot

One 4-inch (10 cm) length of English cucumber

Kosher salt

3 ounces (85 g) Spam

½ to ¾ cup (80 to 120 g) drained canned pineapple chunks

1 handful basil

4 sheets Vietnamese rice paper

4 medium-large whole butter lettuce leaves, plus another 4 to 6 leaves, thinly sliced

1 handful cilantro leaves and thin stems

Store-bought crispy fried shallots or onions (optional)

1 small handful mint leaves

SAUCE

2 tablespoons hoisin sauce

2 tablespoons creamy peanut butter

Traditional Vietnamese gỏi cuốn, known in English as summer rolls or fresh spring rolls, are almost always filled with the same ingredients: rice noodles, pork, shrimp, and fresh herbs. But like many of the world's most brilliant dishes, these healthy snacks have morphed and stretched to accommodate a wide variety of ingredient combinations as they've become popular around the world. You can find Korean versions (wollamssam) that include a range of vegetables and fruit, European versions full of chicken and avocado, and even BLT versions.

This recipe—designed to use only ready-to-eat ingredients that don't require much prep (which meant leaving out the noodles)—takes cues from Hawaii with a sweet-salty combination of Spam and canned pineapple. Add lots and lots of shredded vegetables and a simplified peanut dipping sauce, and these rolls make a light but flavorful meal perfect for a warm summer evening.

Use a fine-toothed mandoline (or a vegetable peeler and a sharp knife) to julienne the carrot and the cucumber. Mix the cucumber with a couple pinches of salt and set it aside. Cut the Spam into very thin strips and sear them over high heat in a nonstick pan, turning them once or twice, until each one is brown on two sides. Cut the pineapple chunks into thin fan-shaped slices and chiffonade the basil. Squeeze any remaining moisture out of the salted cucumber.

CONTINUED

Fill a shallow bowl or rimmed plate with lukewarm water. Dip a sheet of rice paper into the water for about 5 seconds (rotating it in the water if necessary to moisten the whole sheet), then transfer the rice paper to a plate or cutting board.

Lay a leaf of lettuce on the right side of the sheet and fill it with a thick horizontal line of one-fourth of the carrot, cucumber, and Spam; then add a couple big pinches of the fried shallots (if using) and one-fourth of the shredded lettuce, basil, and cilantro, plus a few pieces of pineapple. Roll the lettuce leaf around the fillings to hold them snug and tight, and fold the top and bottom of the leaf in to make a short, fat roll. Wrap the right-hand side of the rice paper over the roll, pulling it slightly as you go to keep it taut, and tuck it under very snugly, so the fillings are held tightly together.

Place a vertical line of pineapple on the flat area of the rice paper, alongside the rolled fillings, and lay some more mint and cilantro on top of the pineapple. Fold the top and bottom 2 inches (5 cm) of the rice paper over the ends of the roll, pulling a bit to tighten. Roll the wrapped filling over the line of pineapple and herbs and keep rolling to use up the rest of the rice paper and form a roll with all the fillings inside; transfer the roll to your dinner plate. Repeat the filling and rolling process three more times with the remaining ingredients.

To make the dipping sauce, mix the hoisin and peanut butter in a small bowl and thin it with a bit of water.

PIMENTO CHEESE & TOMATO FINGER SANDWICHES

½ cup (40 g) grated sharp or extra-sharp cheddar

½ ounce (15 g) cream cheese

1 tablespoon drained canned diced pimentos

2 teaspoons mayonnaise

⅛–¼ teaspoon red pepper flakes or chile crisp

Kosher salt

2 pieces soft white bread

1 medium tomato

Pimento cheese is one of those foods that easily bridges the gap between snack food and meal, as comfortable on a potluck table with crudités as it is on a burger. But there's really no better use of it than a pimento cheese sandwich, where this genius combination of ingredients can take center stage. Here, I also combine it with another classic from the American South—a simple, glorious tomato sandwich. Technically, the difference between a pimento cheese sandwich meant as a meal and one meant as a snack is just in how it's presented: a whole sandwich is a meal, while one cut into small tea sandwiches is a snack. I, obviously, prefer the second approach.

Combine the cheddar, cream cheese, and pimentos in a small bowl and mash everything well with the back of a fork. Add the mayonnaise, red pepper flakes, and a pinch of salt and mix everything into a smooth spread. Taste and adjust the red pepper and salt as needed.

Spread the pimento cheese onto one piece of the bread, then cut the tomato into thick slices and arrange them on the cheese before adding the second piece of bread on top. Carefully cut the sandwich in half, then cut each half lengthwise so you have long, thin quarters for a finger sandwich–style presentation.

Bulk Up the Plate: To make your meal feel like a picnic, enjoy this with fresh vegetable sticks and a handful (or three) of potato chips.

ONIGIRI WITH SMOKED SALMON

¾ cup (150 g) Japanese short-grain white rice

⅓ ounce (10 g) smoked salmon

Himalayan pink salt, or similar

1 sheet sushi nori

Onigiri are absolutely perfect little packages of food: simple, portable, and filling. One makes a hearty snack; two or three are a full meal. In Japan you can pick them up everywhere from convenience stores to kiosks in train stations to dedicated onigiri shops. My friend Sachiko Ormsby often makes big batches when she throws a party, and a while ago she generously taught me how she does it.

For first-time onigiri makers, there are two tricks to the process: The first is cooking the rice to the right firm-tender texture. Sachiko uses a donabe, but you can use a rice cooker or a pot on your stove. The second trick is to apply the right kind of pressure to shape the balls or triangles so that they stick together. That said, the process isn't actually hard, so it won't take you long to get the hang of it.

Rinse the rice well, until the water runs clear, and drain it. Put the rice in a rice cooker or a medium pot with ¾ cup (180 ml) of water. If using a pot, bring the water just to a boil over medium heat, then give the rice a stir to make sure none has started sticking to the bottom (and that it's in a relatively even layer); cover the pot and turn the heat to low. Simmer for 12 minutes, then turn the heat off and let the rice sit undisturbed so that it continues to steam in its own heat for another 10 minutes.

CONTINUED

While the rice is steaming, toast the salmon briefly in a hot nonstick pan over medium heat, flipping it once or twice so that it cooks through and its color lightens. When the rice is ready, use a rice spatula to spread it out on a dinner plate so it can cool slightly, then divide it into roughly equal parts (three, if you have large hands, or four, if you have small hands). Divide the salmon into the same number of portions, and pour a little bit of salt into a small bowl.

When the rice is just cool enough to handle, rinse your hands with water, then dip a finger into the salt and rub it over both your palms. Take most of one section of the rice (all except for about 1 tablespoon) and form it into a patty in one hand. Create a little indent in the top of the patty, put one portion of the salmon in the indent, and cover it with the remaining tablespoon of rice. Using both hands, press the rice into a ball; start with light pressure and then increase the pressure as you turn the ball in your hands a bit.

Once the ball holds together, you can leave the onigiri as is or form it into its distinctive triangle shape: Press the rice ball gently with one hand shaped like a U to form the flat bottom, and one hand creased into a deep V, to form the top corner; rotate the triangle so another corner is facing up and press again. Turn and press the onigiri a few times so all the sides and corners are compressed evenly. Repeat the process with the other portions of rice and salmon.

Cut the nori into three or four strips, depending on the number of onigiri you shaped, and wrap the strips around the balls or triangles before eating.

HALIBUT-AVOCADO CEVICHE WITH COCONUT MILK

½ red Fresno chile

¼ small shallot

¼ cup (60 ml) unsweetened coconut milk

4 ounces (115 g) halibut fillet

2 tablespoons freshly squeezed lime juice

2 tablespoons freshly squeezed grapefruit juice

½ medium avocado, such as Hass or Fuerte

1 small handful of cilantro

Kosher salt

Freshly ground black pepper

Banana or plantain chips

There's pretty much no faster, easier way to "cook" fish than to cure it in a bath of citrus juice, so it's no wonder that people have been making ceviche for centuries. Peru claims this dish as its own—there's evidence that it originated with the Moche people—but now you'll find it all across Latin America. This version takes cues from a variety of different styles and uses a simple dressing made with coconut milk in lieu of the traditional (and more time-consuming) leche de tigre. Using a mix of lime and grapefruit juice to cure the fish gives the dish a more nuanced flavor than just lime alone, while store-bought banana or plantain chips stand in for the fried plantains (patacones) often served on the side.

Thinly slice the chile and shallot and place them in a small bowl. Shake the coconut milk well and add it to the bowl; let the mixture meld while you prepare the fish. Cut the fish into roughly ½-inch (1.3 cm) cubes, and add it to a small bowl with the lime and grapefruit juices. Marinate the fish for 10 to 15 minutes, stirring as necessary to make sure all the pieces cure. Dice the avocado into pieces roughly the same size as the fish cubes; thinly slice the cilantro.

Add the coconut dressing to the fish and citrus juices and season everything with a pinch of salt and a bit of pepper. Stir the avocado pieces into the mixture, add more salt to taste, and sprinkle the cilantro on top. Enjoy with the banana chips: pile bites of ceviche onto them or eat them on the side.

Bulk Up the Plate: Boiled corn and/or wedges of roasted sweet potato are great, traditional companions for ceviche.

PREP-AHEAD SNACKS

Some of the best snacks in the world require a little more patience and time to prepare, but that doesn't mean they can't be ready quickly when you need them; all you have to do is plan ahead.

These recipes break up your dinner prep so that you can tackle the most time-consuming parts whenever it's convenient (in the morning while you eat breakfast, perhaps, or on a slow weekend afternoon), then set the partially prepared meal in your refrigerator to finish up right before you eat. They give you a chance to expand your snacking repertoire to include slightly more complex dishes—and once you have the snacks waiting in your fridge, all ready to go, you'll want to get home to eat them as soon as possible.

MIX & MATCH POTATO BITES

1 pound (450 g) small (new) potatoes

Kosher salt

Medium or sharp cheddar

Beef jerky, salami, or a vegan equivalent

Cornichons

Pickled peppers

Assorted olives

Sun-dried tomatoes

Scallion, white and light-green parts only

Flat-leaf parsley

Avocado

Sour cream

Whole-grain mustard

There's something about a halved baby potato topped with something delicious—a dollop of sour cream, a sliver of avocado, a flurry of fresh herbs—that brings to mind a tray of passed appetizers. These bites make me think of holiday parties at fancy friends' houses with drinks mixed to order and nice cocktail napkins. The key to turning potato bites into a full meal is to serve the little spuds on a platter with lots of different topping options so you can mix and match. Depending on what you add to each, you can end up with a flavor mixture reminiscent of potato skins, German potato salad, or even Cobb salad.

Prep ahead: Put the potatoes into a medium pot with a generous amount of salt. Add enough water to cover the potatoes by about 1 inch (2.5 cm) and bring the water to a boil. Boil the potatoes until they're just tender all the way through, 8 to 10 minutes, then drain them and let them cool. Refrigerate the potatoes in an airtight container for up to 4 days (or use immediately).

Finish the Dish: Finely grate some cheddar; mince some jerky, cornichons, peppers, olives, and sun-dried tomatoes; thinly slice a scallion and chop some parsley; finely dice the avocado. Make piles of each ingredient on one side of a plate and add dollops of sour cream and mustard alongside. Cut each potato in half lengthwise and put them on the other side of the plate. To eat, slick a little sour cream on the cut side of a potato half to act as a binder, then pile on generous amounts of toppings, playing with the mix of flavors.

10

SPICED NUTS, OLIVES & RAISINS ON HUMMUS

HUMMUS

1½ cups (300 g) drained canned or cooked chickpeas (method follows)

1 or 2 garlic cloves

1½ tablespoons tahini

½ teaspoon kosher salt, plus more to taste

¼ teaspoon ground cumin, plus more to taste

I'll admit it: for a long time I thought I didn't like hummus. But that was before I'd had the opportunity to try the homemade stuff. Light and creamy and flavorful, homemade hummus is now one of my favorite snacks—something I make on a weekend and tuck in the fridge to use in countless meals. Here, I top it with raisins, pine nuts, and seasoned olives and pair it with pita and cucumber. (Note: This recipe makes extra hummus, about twice as much as you need for one person, so you can enjoy it a couple of times during the week; it keeps in the fridge for about 5 days.)

Prep Ahead: Transfer the chickpeas to a food processor. Add the garlic, tahini, salt, and cumin, and process everything until it has turned into a very smooth mixture. Taste the hummus and adjust the seasonings as you like. Scrape the sides of the processor bowl and then, with the food processor running, slowly add 1 to 2 tablespoons of water to thin the hummus to your desired texture. Refrigerate the hummus in an airtight container for up to 5 days if not using immediately.

CONTINUED

SPICED TOPPING

1 tablespoon raisins

1 tablespoon sherry vinegar

4 pitted Castelvetrano olives

Pita bread

1 heaping tablespoon pine nuts

1 heaping tablespoon blanched and slivered almonds

1 tablespoon extra-virgin olive oil

¼ teaspoon sweet smoked paprika, plus more to garnish

¼ teaspoon ground cinnamon

⅛ teaspoon ground cumin

Kosher salt

Cucumbers or other vegetables

Finish the Dish: Take the hummus out of the refrigerator so it starts to come to room temperature. Put the raisins in a small bowl with the vinegar and just enough very hot water to fully submerge them, and let them soak for 5 minutes. While the raisins are soaking, cut the olives into thin slices and toast the pita.

Toast the pine nuts and almonds in a small pan over medium heat, stirring frequently. Drain the raisins and, when the nuts are just turning lightly golden, add the raisins and the olives to the pan and cook for about 30 seconds, stirring frequently. Add the olive oil and let everything sizzle for 1 minute; the raisins will puff up and some of the nuts will turn dark brown. Add the paprika, cinnamon, cumin, and a pinch of salt and stir for 30 seconds to toast the spices. Remove the pan from the heat and continue to stir while the mixture cools slightly.

Spoon about half the hummus into a low, wide bowl and use the back of a spoon to make a trough in the middle (refrigerate the rest of the hummus for a later use). Scoop the filling into the trough, then sprinkle on a bit more paprika. Slice the toasted pita into wedges and arrange them and some sliced cucumber or other vegetables on the side.

SOFT-COOKED CHICKPEAS

¾ cup (150 g) dried chickpeas

1½ teaspoons baking soda

Kosher salt

Put the chickpeas in a bowl with 1 teaspoon of the baking soda (this helps soften their skins and makes them more digestible). Add enough water to allow the chickpeas to double in size, and let them soak overnight.

Drain the soaked chickpeas, rinse them briefly under running water, and transfer them to a medium-large pot. Add the remaining ½ teaspoon of baking soda, a pinch of salt, and enough water to cover the chickpeas by at least 4 inches (10 cm). Bring to a boil, then lower the temperature to medium-low, skim off any scum that has risen to the surface, and simmer the chickpeas until they are soft (even a little mushy), about 1 hour.

SHIRO MITTEN DIP WITH INJERA CHIPS & BELL PEPPER

1 tablespoon bessobela

¼ cup (60 ml) vegetable oil

2 tablespoons roughly chopped tomato

1 heaping tablespoon finely chopped red onion

2 teaspoons minced jalapeño

2 teaspoons minced garlic

1 teaspoon kosher salt

½ cup (70 g) shiro mitten powder

Store-bought injera chips

Red bell pepper, seeded and cut into strips

This dish is rich and complex but quite easy to make; most of the flavor comes from shiro mitten powder—a mix of toasted chickpea flour, berbere, bessobela (sacred basil), and other spices—that you can buy premade at Ethiopian markets. Every version of the mix is different (and every mix has a different level of spiciness).

This shiro mitten recipe is adapted from the version made by Fetlework Tefferi, the owner of Brundo Spice Company, and is the same one you'll get if you visit her beloved Oakland restaurant, Cafe Colucci. Tefferi originally started Brundo as a way to source high-quality ingredients for the restaurant, but ended up expanding her business so that Ethiopian American cooks (and others) could have access to fresh, well-sourced ingredients. Today, Brundo sells a variety of Ethiopian ingredients, all made using traditional processing methods, including the shiro mitten powder and bessobela used in this recipe.

Prep Ahead: Bring 1 cup (240 ml) of water to a boil in a small pot and add the bessobela, then lower the heat to maintain a simmer and cook until about three-quarters of the water has boiled away and what remains is like a brownish-red tea, about 10 minutes; set the pot aside.

While the bessobela is infusing, heat the vegetable oil in a nonreactive pan and add the tomato, onion, jalapeño, garlic, and salt. Cook, stirring pretty constantly, until everything is very soft and the onions have started to brown, 1 or 2 minutes. Add 1½ cups (360 ml) of water to the vegetable mixture and bring to a boil. Add the shiro mitten powder to the pan and cook, stirring to create a uniform mixture and break up clumps, until the spices are toasted and the flour has cooked through, about 2 minutes. Strain the bessobela-infused water through a fine-mesh sieve into the pan, discarding the leaves, and stir everything together. Remove the shiro mitten from the heat and let it come to room temperature. Refrigerate for up to 3 days if not using immediately.

Finish the Meal: To reheat the shiro, transfer it to a small pot or pan, add enough water to thin it to the texture of a thick porridge, and heat it over medium until it thickens a bit, then transfer it to a small bowl. Arrange the injera chips and bell pepper on the side to scoop up the shiro.

CRISPY RICE & CHORIZO WITH HERBS & LETTUCE

¾ cup (160 g) jasmine rice

3 tablespoons vegetable oil

1½ ounces (45 g) pre-sliced cured (Spanish-style) chorizo

1 stalk lemongrass (optional)

1 small handful mint leaves

1 scallion, white and light-green parts only

1 large handful cilantro

½ a Persian cucumber, or a 2-inch (5 cm) length of English cucumber

1 teaspoon Vietnamese fish sauce

2 teaspoons freshly squeezed lime juice

Romaine lettuce leaves, from the center of the head

Chopped roasted peanuts (optional)

The top of the tahdig, the socarrat in the paella, the bottom of a pot of Mexican rice: that's the part I want. So you won't be surprised to hear that nam khao—the Thai and Lao dish of crispy fried rice often eaten in a lettuce leaf with fresh herbs—is one of my absolute favorite foods. This recipe (shown in the photo on page 9) is inspired by that classic, but I make it without deep-frying the rice. I also add Spanish chorizo, for a flavor reminiscent of the fusion-y chorizo larb at the delightful restaurant Lil' Deb's Oasis in Hudson, New York. (Note: If you have at least 1½ cups [250 g] of leftover rice, you can skip the prep step.)

Prep Ahead: Rinse the rice well, until the water runs clear, and drain it. Put the rice in a rice cooker or a medium pot with ¾ cup plus 3 tablespoons (225 ml) of water. If using a pot, bring the water just to a boil over high heat, then give the rice a stir to make sure none has started sticking to the bottom (and that it's in a relatively even layer), cover the pot, and turn the heat to low. Simmer the rice for 20 minutes, then turn the heat off and let the rice sit, undisturbed, so that it continues to steam in its own heat for another 10 minutes. Refrigerate the rice for at least 1 night and up to 5 days. (You may end up with a bit more rice than you need for the recipe, depending on how it cooks.)

Finish the Meal: Mix 1½ cups (250 g) of the cooked rice with the oil, breaking up any chunks so every grain is coated. Finely mince the chorizo (you'll have a scant ¼ cup), and mix it into the rice. Peel the outer leaves off the lemongrass (if using), crush the root end of the stalk using the blunt edge of a cleaver or a pestle. Cut off the firm end of the stalk and finely mince the (relatively) tender yellow/white and purple section of leaves that make up the lower 1 to 2 inches (3 to 5 cm) of the stalk. Thinly slice the mint, scallion, cilantro, and cucumber and combine them in a medium bowl; add ½ tablespoon of the lemongrass (if using), and reserve the rest.

Heat a large nonstick pan over medium-high heat, then add the rice mixture and spread it out, patting it down to make the thinnest layer possible. Turn the heat to medium and cook until the bottom of the rice is golden brown and crispy, 3 to 5 minutes. (If the layer of rice is thick enough that the top of the rice doesn't cook and become crispy in this time, flip the rice and continue frying until it's crispy; if the rice starts to pop out of the pan, cover it with a lid.)

Remove the crispy rice from the pan, leaving behind any excess oil from the chorizo, add it to the bowl of herbs, and mix everything well. Stir the fish sauce and lime juice together in a small bowl or jar and use it to dress the rice and herbs, mixing well. Add another big pinch of lemongrass, if using. To eat, pile bites of the rice mixture into lettuce leaves, adding chopped peanuts if you like.

SWEET & SPICY CHILLED SESAME NOODLES

CHICKEN

1 boneless, skinless chicken thigh

Extra-virgin olive oil

Kosher salt

Freshly ground black pepper

NOODLES

3 ounces (85 g) thin rice noodles, such as Chinese mixian or small Vietnamese rice sticks

2 teaspoons toasted sesame oil

While noodles might not sound like a snacking food to most people, the rich and flavorful mian, mixian, and liang fen made in China's Sichuan Province are often just that—hearty mini-meals full of spicy, sweet, and/or numbing flavors.

This Sichuan-style dish was developed with the team from Fly by Jing, a modern Chinese food company founded by Chengdu native Jing Gao that's best known for its Sichuan Chili Crisp. It's incredibly versatile—you can swap out the traditional sesame paste for another nut butter or use pretty much any leftover protein—and the noodles and chicken can be prepped a few days ahead of time.

Prep Ahead: Put a medium pot of water on to boil and preheat the oven to 425°F (220°C).

Put the chicken thigh on a foil-lined baking sheet, brush it with olive oil, and season it with a generous amount of salt and pepper. Roast the chicken until it reaches 165°F (74°C), 15 to 20 minutes.

When the water comes to a boil, cook the rice noodles until tender, according to the directions on the package (generally 5 to 10 minutes). Drain the noodles, rinse them under cold water until cool, then toss them with the sesame oil.

When the chicken is done, let it sit for a few minutes until it's cool enough to handle, then pull it into long, thin shreds.

Refrigerate the noodles and the chicken for up to 4 days if not using immediately.

CONTINUED

SWEET & SPICY CHILLED SESAME NOODLES, CONTINUED

SAUCE

2 tablespoons Chinese sesame paste

1 tablespoon Japanese soy sauce (such as Kikkoman)

1 tablespoon Chinese black vinegar (such as Shaanxi vinegar)

1 tablespoon dark brown sugar

3 to 5 teaspoons chile crisp (depending on desired heat)

1 garlic clove

TOPPINGS

One 2-inch (5 cm) length of English or Chinese cucumber

Cilantro, mint, and scallion (white and light-green parts only), to garnish

Toasted sesame seeds, to garnish

Mix the sesame paste, soy sauce, vinegar, sugar, chile crisp, and 1 tablespoon of water together in a small bowl. Mince the garlic, add it to the bowl, and mix everything into a relatively smooth sauce. Refrigerate the sauce for up to 4 days as needed.

Finish the Dish: Slice or grate the cucumber into long, thin strips; roughly chop the cilantro and mint; and thinly slice the scallion. Mix the sauce with the chilled noodles, then top them with the chicken, cucumber, and herbs. Sprinkle with some sesame seeds, and mix everything well before eating.

DECONSTRUCTED WINTER FRUIT FATTOUSH

PITA CHIPS

2 thick, pocket-style pitas

Extra-virgin olive oil

Kosher salt

Za'atar

SALAD

½ romaine heart

1 Persian cucumber or a 4-inch (10 cm) length of English cucumber

1 medium tangerine or 2 or 3 small tangerines

10 to 12 mint leaves

2 packed tablespoons flat-leaf parsley

1½ ounces (45 g) feta

3 tablespoons pomegranate arils

1½ tablespoons freshly squeezed lemon juice

1½ tablespoons extra-virgin olive oil

¾ teaspoon pomegranate molasses

Kosher salt

Za'atar

My cousin Hannah once made a dinner for me that was basically a big chopped salad served with tortilla chips instead of forks—a choice that essentially turned the salad into a dip. That meal was the inspiration for this take on fattoush. Since most pita chips can be very thick and hard (a bit overwhelming as a vehicle for salad), I've made my own here, using a technique that makes a thinner version you can store for a couple of days. (Note: This recipe makes more pita chips than you probably need for the salad, but they're great as a snack on their own or as a side element for other snacking dinners like the Spanish Tuna, Tomato & Olive Salad on page 27 or the Crudités with Yogurt-Miso Green Goddess Dip on page 79).

Prep Ahead: Preheat the oven to 400°F (200°C). Cut the pitas in half through the thin edges to make four thinner circles. Lay the circles on a baking sheet, brush them with oil, and season them with salt and za'atar. Bake the pita until crispy, flipping the pieces once (and adding more olive oil and za'atar), about 8 minutes total. Cut the circles into wedges (eight pieces per circle), and let them cool to room temperature. This step can be prepped ahead. Store them in an airtight container for up to 3 days if not using immediately.

CONTINUED

Finish the Meal: Cut the romaine crosswise into very thin slices and then rotate your knife 90 degrees and finely chop the slices. Slice the ends off the cucumber, cut it in half lengthwise, slice each half into very thin strips, then rotate your knife 90 degrees and cut the strips into a very fine dice. Peel the tangerine(s) and separate the segments, removing any very long or thick strings of pith; cut each segment into very small pieces. Mince the mint and parsley, and break the feta into fine crumbles (you'll have about 6 tablespoons' worth). Toss everything together in a medium bowl.

Combine the pomegranate arils, lemon juice, olive oil, and molasses in a jar, add a big pinch salt and a couple of pinches of za'atar, and shake well. Add most of the dressing to the salad, then taste and add more if you like. To eat, use the toasted pita to scoop up big bites of the salad.

Bulk Up the Plate: This makes a pretty filling meal, but if you really want to add something, a Salt & Spice or Saturday Bagel jammy egg (page 71) would complement the salad's flavors and add additional protein.

BUTTERNUT FLATBREAD PULAAR

7½ ounces (215 g) peeled and seeded butternut squash

Extra-virgin olive oil

Kosher salt

Freshly ground black pepper

½ small yellow onion

1 tablespoon za'atar

2 tablespoons freshly squeezed lemon juice

1 large, thick, pocket-style pita (about 8 inches / 20 cm across)

1 large handful salted toasted pumpkin seeds

¼ cup (35 g) crumbled feta

½ teaspoon ground sumac

Chile flakes

1 tablespoon pomegranate arils or dried barberries

Chef Nafy Flatley of Teranga restaurant in San Francisco designed this Senegalese-style flatbread to honor the Arabic influence on her country's cuisine. The base ingredient, butternut squash, stands in for similar hard squashes that grow across West Africa, while the flatbread and za'atar seasoning nod to flavors introduced by trans-Saharan trade with North African communities. While this snack has a few elements that need to be cooked separately before you assemble it, the majority of the work can be done ahead of time; you can even make big batches of the squash and onion and freeze individual portions so they're ready whenever you want them. In fact, Nafy often assembles a few of these flatbreads in a big batch, then freezes them whole so she can heat and serve them in just 15 minutes.

Prep Ahead: Preheat the oven to 400°F (200°C). Cut the butternut squash into approximately ½-inch (1.3 cm) cubes; you should have about 1½ cups. Mix the squash pieces with enough olive oil to thoroughly coat them, then season them with a little salt and a very generous amount of pepper. Mix everything well and transfer the squash to a parchment-lined sheet pan, spreading the pieces out so they aren't clumped together. Roast the squash for 10 minutes, stir and flip the pieces, then roast for another 10 minutes. The squash should have lots of well-browned bits but should not start to burn. Transfer the squash to a small bowl and mash it with the back of a fork until you have a relatively smooth paste.

CONTINUED

While the squash is roasting, cut the onion into ¼-inch (6 mm) slices. Add a thin layer of olive oil to the bottom of a pan and place over high heat until the oil starts to shimmer. Add the onion and cook, stirring constantly, until nearly all the slices are nicely browned along the edges; the smaller pieces may be quite dark. Turn the heat to low, add 2 tablespoons of water to the pan, and continue cooking until the slices are very soft, about 5 minutes (add a little more water if the onion sticks).

Mix the za'atar with the lemon juice, then drizzle in 1 tablespoon of olive oil and mix well. Let the za'atar dressing sit for at least 20 minutes before using. Refrigerate the squash, onions, and dressing for up to 4 days if not using immediately.

Finish the Dish: Preheat the oven to 400°F (200°C). Put the pita on a parchment-lined sheet pan and spread the squash puree on it in an even layer, almost all the way to the edges. Distribute the onion over the squash, sprinkle on the pumpkin seeds, and top with the feta. Bake the flatbread until the cheese starts to brown in places, about 10 minutes. When it is done, drizzle on the za'atar dressing and sprinkle on the sumac and some chile, to taste. To eat, cut the flatbread in half and cut each half into strips, then sprinkle the pomegranate arils over everything.

CORN & SPINACH TOFU BANCHAN

½ cup (100 g) jasmine rice

1 tablespoon millet or amaranth (optional)

4 ounces (115 g) spinach

½ ear corn, shucked

1 scallion

Rice vinegar

1 small garlic clove

Kosher salt

Freshly ground black pepper

½ teaspoon toasted sesame oil

4½ ounces (130 g) firm tofu

2 teaspoons toasted sesame seeds

Water kimchi or dill pickle

Toasted seaweed

Korean banchan—small side dishes of kimchi, cooked vegetables, tiny anchovies, chilled meats, and other flavorful bites—are usually served alongside a larger meal, but the flavors in a banchan spread are so varied and delicious that they can really make a dinner all on their own. This dish (dooboo moochiim) is adapted from one made by Chef Steve Joo at Joodooboo, a small restaurant and shop in Oakland that specializes in handmade tofu and offers a selection of seasonal banchan. If you order one of the restaurant's main dishes, the banchan will come on the side, but you can also just get a banchan set and some of the tofu and enjoy it all together.

Because this particular banchan includes both vegetables and tofu, it can basically make a meal on its own with some rice, but in the spirit of this style of meal, you'll want to have at least one or two more items with it, like a mild water kimchi and maybe some gim (toasted seaweed). All the elements can be prepared a couple of days ahead and refrigerated, then combined quickly before you eat. (Note: If it's not peak corn season, you can add a pinch of sugar to bring up the flavor.)

Prep Ahead: Rinse the rice well, until the water runs clear, then transfer it to a small bowl, along with the millet (if using). Add warm water to cover, let the rice soak for 10 minutes, then drain it. Put the rice in a rice cooker or a medium pot with ½ cup (120 ml) of water (plus 1 tablespoon if using the millet). If using a pot, bring the water just to a boil over medium heat, then give the rice a stir to make sure none has started sticking to the bottom; cover the pot and turn the heat to low. Simmer the rice for 12 minutes, then turn the heat off and let the rice sit, undisturbed, so that it continues to steam in its own heat, for another 10 minutes. Refrigerate for up to 5 days if not using immediately.

While the rice is cooking, bring a medium pot of water to a boil. Combine ice cubes and cold tap water in a bowl to make an ice bath. Separate the spinach leaves from any thick stems. When the water boils, put the thick stems in and cook them until tender, 2 to 3 minutes, then add the leaves and blanch them for a few seconds; use tongs to transfer all the greens to the ice bath to cool. Broil the corn, turning as needed, until it is lightly browned on all sides (the timing will vary depending on your oven). While the corn is cooking, drain the spinach, squeeze out all the excess moisture, and finely chop. Cut the kernels off the corn and combine it with the spinach. Store in the refrigerator for up to 4 days if not using immediately.

Finish the Dish: Remove the vegetables from the refrigerator, if needed, and allow them to come to room temperature. Thinly slice the white and light-green parts of the scallion (reserve the dark-green parts), and put the slices in a small bowl with enough rice vinegar to cover; set it aside to pickle lightly while you cook. Thinly slice the dark-green part of the scallion and add it to the vegetables. Crush the garlic with ¼ teaspoon of salt (mashing and scraping it into a paste with the side of a knife or pestle), add it to the vegetables with a tiny bit of black pepper, and massage everything together. Drizzle in the sesame oil and mix everything well with your hands.

Crumble the tofu into a separate bowl. Lightly crush the sesame seeds, then add them, the pickled scallion, and ¼ teaspoon of the pickling vinegar to the tofu with ¼ teaspoon of salt; mix well. Combine the vegetable mixture and the tofu mixture and mix well (again, your hands will work best); taste and adjust the seasonings as necessary. Reheat the rice and pile the banchan on it, with some of the kimchi or pickle and seaweed on the side.

Bulk Up the Plate: To add more heft and variety to your meal, add a Bartavelle or Shortcut Banchan jammy egg (page 71); or, if you have it, some leftover roast chicken.

SPLURGY SNACKS

These snacks are for the nights when you want a decadent treat, when you're looking for a simple but delicious way to celebrate a birthday, a promotion, a holiday, or a personal accomplishment. (Conversely, they're also perfect when the universe is not on your side and you need to balance out a bad day by treating yourself really well.)

They are all quite simple to throw together, but each one revolves around a splurgy ingredient that you would normally only enjoy on a special occasion—and suggests the radical idea that you should eat a lot of it yourself instead of sharing teeny-tiny bites with a whole room of other people. (Plus, if you buy only enough for one person, these more-expensive ingredients won't break the bank the way they would if you got enough for a crowd.) These aren't the recipes you'll turn to regularly, but you should keep them in your back pocket for when you want something fancy and over-the-top for dinner.

CAVIAR SANDWICH

2 pieces Wonder bread or other soft white presliced bread

2 chives

3 tablespoons mild chèvre

About 1 tablespoon sour cream

⅛ teaspoon Colman's mustard powder

⅛ teaspoon garlic powder

1 ounce (30 g) caviar, such as American sturgeon or hackleback, or even whitefish

This sandwich might just be the most decadent snacking meal ever, but if you've bought a tiny, expensive jar of caviar for a holiday celebration and only been able to snag one or two small bites, you'll understand its appeal! Inspired by a sandwich served at New York's Madeline's Martini (usually alongside one of their namesake drinks), this version is designed to showcase the caviar and not overwhelm its flavor. The other ingredients are simple and mild, and I always make it on Wonder bread, which has the right touch of sweetness and the ideal soft-crisp texture when it's toasted (and let's be honest, you're not making this sandwich because you want a healthy, well-rounded meal). Brioche would also work well.

Lightly toast the bread, and thinly slice the chives. Mix the chèvre with enough sour cream to make the cheese spreadable in a small bowl and mix in the mustard powder, garlic powder, and chives, then spread half the mixture on each of the pieces of toast. Spread the entire ounce of caviar onto one slice, on top of the cheese mixture, then gently place the other slice of bread on top. Carefully cut the sandwich in half or into quarters, using a serrated knife to saw through the toast so you don't have to press down and force the caviar out the sides.

Bulk Up the Plate: If you find affordable caviar (or have deep pockets), you might want to double this whole thing and make two sandwiches for a full meal. Alternatively, this would be great paired with roasted nuts, crudités, and a Not-Quite-Deviled jammy egg (page 71).

UNSTUFFED CRAB & AVOCADO

2 ounces (60 g) picked crabmeat

1 tablespoon finely chopped celery

1 tablespoon mayonnaise

½ teaspoon thinly sliced chives

Kosher salt

Freshly ground pepper

1 tangerine and 1 Meyer lemon, for zesting and juice

½ large or 1 small avocado

1 kumquat, thinly sliced, seeds removed (optional)

Ritz crackers

As a Californian who grew up surrounded by avocado orchards and eating locally sourced crab, I assumed that the classic mid-century dish of half an avocado stuffed with crab salad had been created in my home state. But it turns out that cooks all over the Americas have been piling ingredients into avocado halves for over a century, and that the version with crab salad was invented in Louisiana in the 1940s. Wherever this dish came from, it's one of my absolute favorite foods. Here, I've turned this appetizer into a snack by slicing up the avocado so that it and the crab can be piled onto Ritz crackers. I've also added some citrus for a California twist.

Mix the crabmeat with the celery, mayonnaise, and chives in a small bowl; season with a pinch of salt and a grind of pepper. Grate a little tangerine zest and Meyer lemon zest directly into the bowl (with a microplane or the zesting side of a box grater). Pit the avocado and peel away the skin. Cut the flesh into thin slices, fan it out on a plate, and season with a squeeze of Meyer lemon juice and a pinch of salt. Pile the crab salad next to or on top of the avocado and sprinkle everything with the kumquat slices (if using). To eat, use the Ritz crackers as a base for big bites of crab and avocado.

PÂTÉ BANH MI BITES

2½ ounces (70 g) creamy duck liver pâté, or similar

¾ cup (120 g) peeled and grated daikon

2 tablespoons grated carrot

Kosher salt

4¼ teaspoons granulated sugar

¼ cup (60 ml) distilled white vinegar

½ a baguette

1 small jalapeño

1 handful cilantro

The French legacy in Vietnam includes some delicious cultural mash-ups, but for my money, none is more delicious than banh mi. The combination of French bread and pâté with traditional Vietnamese meats, pickles, herbs, and chiles is pure genius. This snack is a simplified version of banh mi, using just pâté (with no other meats) and assembled bite by bite, so you can balance all the flavors as you like. To make it faster, I speed up the process of making the pickles by grating the daikon and carrot on the side of a box grater so that they absorb the vinegar more quickly.

Set the pâté on a plate to let it come to room temperature.

Combine the daikon and carrot in a small bowl with a big pinch of salt and ¼ teaspoon of the sugar and massage with your fingers for 1 minute so the salt and sugar start to penetrate the vegetables and they lose some of their water. Transfer the vegetables to a fine-mesh strainer, rinse them with cool water, and press out any excess moisture. Combine the vinegar and remaining 4 teaspoons of sugar with 3 tablespoons of hot water in a small bowl and stir until the sugar dissolves. Add the vegetables to this brine and let them sit for 10 minutes.

While the vegetables are pickling, slice the baguette and cut the jalapeño into very thin circles. Arrange the bread, jalapeño, and cilantro on a plate with the pâté, and when the pickle is ready, drain the liquid away and pile the pickle on the plate. To eat, spread some pâté on a piece of baguette, top it with a thatch of pickle, and garnish with a little bit of jalapeño and cilantro.

Bulk Up the Plate: This dish is savory and has a very soft texture, so add a sweet or crunchy snack like grapes or mango or some kettle chips.

PÂTÉ DE CAMPAGNE WITH BAGUETTE & PICKLES

⅓ of a baguette

4 ounces (115 g) rustic country-style pâté (pâté de campagne)

Cornichons and other pickled vegetables

Pickled onions (recipe follows)

Whole-grain mustard

According to Julia Child, all you need to make pâté into a meal is some bread and a salad. While a few leaves of lettuce (dressed with equal parts vinegar, Dijon mustard, and olive oil) would be lovely with this dish, they're not actually necessary. When you want to keep things simple, all you need is a slice of country-style pâté (the kind made with coarse pieces of meat) with some pickled vegetables and a punchy glass of wine.

Slice the baguette or cut it in half lengthwise, and arrange the pieces on a plate with the pâté and the pickles and onions. Put a dollop of mustard on the edge of the plate. To eat, spread a bite's worth of pâté and a bit of mustard onto a piece of baguette and top it with a sliver or two of onion; alternate with bites of pickle.

Bulk Up the Plate: If you want to add some vegetables to the plate, you can make a quick salad, Julia Child–style (see head note), or you can add another classic French appetizer: mild breakfast radishes with softened butter, sprinkled with a little fleur de sel.

FASTEST PICKLED ONIONS

⅛ medium red onion

½ teaspoon kosher salt

2 tablespoons apple cider or red wine vinegar

Granulated sugar

Cut the onion into very thin slices and put it into a small bowl with the salt. Massage the salt into the onion slices, then let them sit for 5 minutes. When the onion slices have wilted, rinse them briefly, then put them back into the bowl with the vinegar, a pinch of sugar, and a tablespoon of water. (Add more vinegar and water in a 2:1 ratio as needed to just cover the onion.) Let everything sit for 10 minutes to pickle. Refrigerate the pickled onions for up to 3 weeks if not using immediately.

TUNA & PLUM POKE BOWL

½ cup (100 g) Japanese short-grain rice

4 ounces (115 g) sushi-grade tuna

1 medium plum or ½ medium smooth-fleshed mango, plus more for garnish (optional)

1 scallion, white and light-green parts only

½ large shiso leaf or 1 basil leaf, plus more for garnish (optional)

1 teaspoon Japanese soy sauce (such as Kikkoman)

½ teaspoon mirin

¼ teaspoon toasted sesame oil

¼ teaspoon chile crisp, plus more as needed

¼ teaspoon toasted sesame seeds

1 tablespoon crispy fried shallots or onions (store-bought)

In Hawaii, poke is an everyday treat, something you can buy premade in grocery stores or pick up at a food truck. In other parts of the world, however, fresh sushi-grade fish is often harder to come by—but totally worth the splurge. This maximalist poke pairs ruby-red tuna with sweet-sour summer plums and lots of herbs—plus chile crisp and some crispy fried shallots. Adding all these extras to the gorgeous fish is kind of gilding the lily, but the result is flavorful and fun.

Rinse the rice well, until the water runs clear, and drain it. Put the rice in a rice cooker or a medium pot with ½ cup (120 ml) of water. If using a pot, bring the water just to a boil over medium heat, then give the rice a stir to make sure none has started sticking to the bottom, cover the pot, and turn the heat to low. Simmer the rice for 12 minutes, then turn the heat off and let the rice sit and steam in its own heat for 10 minutes.

While the rice is cooking, dice the tuna into ½-inch (1.3 cm) cubes, and cut the plum into cubes of about the same size (or a touch smaller). Thinly slice the scallion and chiffonade the shiso. Put the fish, plum, and scallion in a small bowl, drizzle in the soy sauce, mirin, sesame oil, and chile crisp and mix well; taste and adjust the seasonings as needed. Stir in the sesame seeds and shiso, sprinkle everything with the shallot, and enjoy immediately over the rice garnished with more plum and shiso, if you like.

BAKED BRIE WITH TRUFFLE SAUCE

One 8- to 9½-ounce (225 to 270 g) round of Brie, packaged in a wooden box

1 scallion, white and light-green parts only

1 sweet-tart apple, such as Fuji or envy

4 or 5 teaspoons tartufata

Kosher salt

Baguette

This is one of the richest snacks ever, the kind of thing you might treat yourself to on a cold winter night for a small personal celebration. First you bake a round of Brie, essentially turning it into a triple-cream fondue. Then you up the ante by stirring in some truffle-infused tartufata, an Italian sauce made from mushrooms, truffles, and (sometimes) olives, mixed together in oil.

Brie comes in a range of sizes, and this recipe will work with the smaller rounds on the market. The important thing is to get one packaged in a circular wooden box, which will help it hold together as it bakes. You'll also want to taste your tartufata to judge how much to add; I prefer Bernardini Tartufi, which has a lovely, fresh flavor and is pretty affordable.

Preheat the oven to 375°F (190°C). While the Brie is very cold, remove any plastic wrapping and cut the white rind off the top, then put the cheese back into the wooden box, cut side up. Put the box on a big square of aluminum foil and fold the sides of the foil up so that it is wrapped tightly around the bottom and sides of the cheese but the top is still uncovered.

Bake the Brie until it is very soft and bubbly, 15 to 20 minutes. Meanwhile, thinly slice the scallion and cut the apple into thick slices. When the Brie is soft and runny, take it out of the oven and top it with the truffle sauce, the scallion, and a large pinch of salt, then stir all the toppings into the cheese. If the Brie firms up when you add the flavorings, return it to the oven for a bit to soften again. When the cheese is done, carefully remove the foil—but only if it's possible to do so without letting the cheese ooze out—and transfer it in its wooden box to a plate. To eat, dip chunks of baguette and slices of apple into the "fondue."

A SNACKER'S PANTRY

The key to a good snacking dinner is having good ingredients: the better your basics, the less actual cooking you need to do to turn them into a delicious meal. If I can plan my snack ahead of time (or while driving home at night), I'll often swing by the market for items like perfectly ripe tomatoes, fresh herbs, or a slice of pâté. But I also keep my kitchen stocked with a variety of shelf-stable and long-lasting ingredients so I can make a quick, delicious meal out of what I already have on hand. Here are the foods I keep on repeat on my shopping list, so I can make a hearty snack whenever I want one.

GOOD CHEESE

What cheese do you reach for when you want something to nibble on? A sharp cheddar? An umami-rich Parmesan? A creamy goat cheese? Whatever it is, that cheese will make the perfect base to build a snacking meal around—and you probably already have it in your fridge. I usually have all three of the cheeses above, along with tubs of shaved Parmesan, which have a long shelf life and can add a lot of rich flavor to everything from pesto (page 26) to Foriana & Parmesan Toasts (page 59).

GOOD BREAD

When I need a last-minute snacking dinner, I head straight to the bread aisle to splurge on something fun and flavorful, like a crunchy baguette or a whole wheat sourdough boule. With good bread, you can make a meal out of anything from charcuterie (page 66) to tinned fish (page 52) to pâté (page 132). If you want to keep the good stuff around all the time, just slice and freeze it; you can pop a piece into the toaster whenever you're feeling snackish.

RUSTIC CRACKERS

A good cracker can make the difference between a bland bite and a flavorful snack. The best crackers for most applications have lots of flavor on their own and can hold up to having ingredients spread or piled on top (I'm not a fan of anything that breaks as soon as I try to spread some soft cheese on it). Ak-Mak crackers work really well with lots of different toppings, thanks to their sturdiness and healthy flavor, while specialty brands like the Fine Cheese Co. (from England) and Yiayia and Friends (from Greece) offer options that make a snacking plate feel a little bit special.

GOOD OLIVE OIL

We often treat (and sell) olive oil like a commodity—as if it were a product like ketchup that is essentially the same in every bottle. But olive oil is an agricultural product, like juice, and its flavor can vary wildly depending on the type of olives it's made with and how it's processed and stored. These differences can, in turn, have a huge impact on the foods you cook: an unexpectedly bitter oil can overwhelm a salad dressing while an old (rancid) oil will add "off" flavors to everything you cook.

The key is to find an oil that you trust, and use it for most of your cooking. I like to use Seka Hills' arbequina oil, both because it has a lovely, mild flavor that goes well in every application and because it's local to where I live; also, the company's profits support the Yocha Dehe Wintun Nation, a Native community working to reclaim their historical lands.

KOSHER SALT AND SEA SALT

Table salt, kosher salt, and sea salts all react differently in food, and each has a different level of salinity. In fact, the two most readily available brands of kosher salt, Diamond and Morton, have completely different shapes, and one is twice as salty, by volume, as the other. **The recipes in this book primarily use Diamond Crystal kosher salt**, because it dissolves quickly in anything you add it to. If you use Morton salt, cut the measurements given here in half. And always make sure to taste your food before and after you salt it. I also keep some flaky sea salt, like Maldon, on hand for finishing dishes at the table.

LOTS OF PICKLES

Dill spears, cornichons, kimchi, pickled carrots and fennel, pepperoncini, capers, Chinese suancai—if you look in the back of my refrigerator, you'll see that I like to keep all kinds of vinegary, salted, and fermented treats on hand. A good pickle can add just the right amount of brightness or sweet-sour heat to a dish, or round out the flavors of a snacking plate. And they keep indefinitely at cold temperatures, so there's no reason not to have all your favorites on hand.

OLIVES

Like pickles, olives keep for a long time and can add a bright burst of flavor to a wide variety of foods. I always have some Castelvetranos in my fridge—their meaty texture and mild flavor make them great for a variety of applications. I also often have pimento-stuffed olives and purple varieties like kalamatas. (There's probably even a can of sliced black olives lurking in my cabinet, ready to go for nachos.)

VEGETABLES FOR CRUDITÉS

The easiest way to ensure that you always have something fresh and healthy to snack on is to add celery, carrots, cucumber, and grape (or cherry) tomatoes to your shopping list and keep replenishing them, even if you don't know when you're going to use them. (Hints: Use carrots and celery that are starting to look old to make a flavorful base for soups and tomato-based pasta sauces; pop tomatoes and cucumber slices into your lunch bag.) If you're planning to eat your veggies raw, it's also worth investing a few extra cents to get slightly tastier varieties, like sweet-tender Nantes carrots and dense, flavorful English or Persian cucumbers.

HIGH-QUALITY TINNED SEAFOOD

Whether you pop them onto crackers (page 48) or eat them as part of a Spanish tapas (page 52), good tinned fish or other types of seafood make a perfect main for a really easy and delicious snacking meal. I almost always have some sardines in the house, and I also try to keep something fun on hand, like Spanish mussels or octopus. Some of my favorite options include anything by Fishwife Tinned Seafood Co. (a woman-founded company that prioritizes sustainable fisheries) as well as Matiz and Porto Muiños (both great sources for Spanish conservas).

OTHER PRESERVED PROTEINS

Like tinned fish, good preserved meats—Italian salami, Spanish cured chorizo, and even high-quality jerky—can keep in your cabinet or the back of your refrigerator for quite a while. Break them out whenever you need a no-cook protein or a flavor boost for meals like nachos (page 85) or beans on toast (page 51).

CANNED BEANS

Keep a few cans of beans stashed in the back of a cupboard, and you can have a hearty dinner ready in minutes. While I often cook dried beans from scratch, I always have at least one can each of black beans, pinto beans, and white beans (like cannellinis) in my pantry; they've saved me from dinner-hour panic more times than I can count.

ASSORTED NUTS

Need to add some protein to your meal without adding to your cooking time? Just pour some of your favorite nuts into a bowl and stick it in the middle of your table. It doesn't matter what kind you get, as long as it's something you can nibble on endlessly. If you like having pine nuts around to add to things like pesto (page 26), keep them in the fridge; they go rancid faster than other nuts.

DRIED FRUIT

To add a sweet (but healthy) note to your snacks, keep some dried fruit on hand. A selection of raisins, dried mango, apricots, and cranberries (and maybe even some things like dried figs or banana chips) will come in handy when you want something sweet with your meal, or to make a sweet-savory snack (page 55).

HIGH-QUALITY SPICES & SPICE MIXTURES

A well-stocked spice drawer is a snacker's secret weapon. Good spice mixes (like shichimi togarashi and za'atar) and some fun basics (like garlic powder and Aleppo pepper) offer the easiest way to add flavor to pretty much anything, turning tubs of plain yogurt into delicious dips and boiled eggs into delightful bites.

FLAVOR BOOSTERS

To take your snacks to the next level, invest in a few tubs and jars of umami-rich ingredients like miso, gochujang, seasoned mayonnaise (like Kewpie), and Worcestershire sauce. Just a little dollop or a few drops of these will add richness and depth to anything you're cooking, from cocktail sauce (page 93) to green goddess dip (page 80). (See the Global Pantry Glossary on page 146 for more about these and other ingredients.)

SPICY DRIZZLES

Nothing jazzes up a quick snack like a little bit of spiciness—especially if the heat also comes with a lot of flavor. You can get this boost from your favorite hot sauce (like Tabasco or Tapatío), or turn to any of the Chinese-style chile crisps and Mexican salsa machas on the market. I have all of these in my fridge at all times (I'm particularly partial to Fly by Jing Chili Crisp), as well as a little bottle of yuzu kosho, which, while not exactly a drizzle, also adds a delicious, flavorful heat to anything that could use a little hint of citrus flavor. (See the Global Pantry Glossary on page 146 for more about these and other ingredients.)

SNACKING TOOLS

Before we dive into a discussion of tools, a quick note: The best thing you can do to make cooking easy is to **keep your knives sharp**! If you're not used to sharpening your knives, it may seem daunting, but if you use something like a pocket knife sharpener or a Lansky C-Sharp ceramic knife sharpener (both of which are cheap and quite small), the process is basically foolproof. Now on to the tools:

Making snacking meals doesn't require any tools that you wouldn't use for all your regular, everyday cooking. The ones I used most often when making these recipes were a **sharp knife**, a **cutting board**, and standard **measuring implements** (as an American cook, I use measuring cups and spoons, but I also have a good kitchen scale because it makes some measuring tasks a million times easier). I also used my **broiler** and **toaster oven** a lot to quickly melt cheeses and lightly cook other ingredients, a **food processor** to make sauces and dips, and both a **box grater** and a **microplane zester** for shredding cheeses and other ingredients. For stovetop cooking, I used a small or medium **pot** or **pan**.

That said, if you are going to be making meals for one regularly (or are preparing a bunch of single servings separately), there are a few things that will make the process easier—and more fun:

Quarter-sheet pan: A sheet pan is different from a cookie sheet in that it has rims on all four sides. The size home cooks usually use—the kind that fits well in home ovens—is technically called a half-sheet pan (only caterers really use the full-sheet version). But to make meals for one, you might want to invest in the even smaller quarter-sheet pan. These little guys (about 9 by 13 inches / 23 by 33 cm) are far lighter and easier to pull in and out of your broiler compartment, will keep smaller volumes of ingredients from sliding around much, and may even fit in your toaster oven, depending on its size.

Small baking dishes: Smaller baking dishes, sometimes sold as "gratin dishes," are roughly 9 inches / 23 cm long (if oval) or 9 inches / 23 cm square. Like quarter-sheet pans, they keep smaller amounts of ingredients grouped together so their flavors meld and their juices don't spread out and evaporate. Brands like Staub make colorful ceramic versions that can come right to the table to serve as your dining plate (just be careful when they're hot!).

Small cheeseboard: Nothing makes a meal feel snacky and fun like arranging it on a decorative board. Any nonreactive tray will do (I often use my cute quarter-sheet pans), but a good wooden cheese board or melamine tray sized for one (about 9 to 15 inches / 23 to 38 cm long) will make your meal feel even more special.

Ramekins and small bowls: If you're making dip for a crowd, any serving bowl will do. But if you're making just enough for yourself, a ramekin or a pretty dessert-size bowl will be invaluable. Most 4-ounce (120 ml) ramekins come in sets of six, so you'll always have one on hand whenever you need to serve yourself a dip or corral nuts or olives on a cheeseboard.

GLOBAL PANTRY GLOSSARY

The recipes in this book use a variety of flavorful ingredients from all across the world. You're likely to find many of these ingredients (from all culinary traditions) in larger supermarkets, but some might require a trip to a specialty store or just a willingness to order a few things online. Here's a quick primer to help with your shopping.

Aleppo pepper: Deeply flavorful and with a very mild heat, this spice is named for the Syrian city of Aleppo but is now mostly produced in neighboring countries like Turkey. It has a deep burgundy color and a nuanced flavor and can be found in Middle Eastern markets and most large supermarkets.

bessobela: This Ethiopian herb, often called "sacred basil," is actually made from the purple flowers of a variety of Ethiopian basil, which are separated from the leaves and stems and then dried to concentrate and preserve their unique flavor. It can be found in African markets and through online retailers like Brundo Spice Company.

boondi and sev: These crispy, crunchy bits made from chickpea flour or lentils and seasoned with chile and spices are two of the key ingredients in many chaat recipes. Boondi are shaped like tiny balls, sev like noodle shards; both are readily available in South Asian markets and also easy to buy online.

chaat masala: This masala (spice mix) is specifically made for sprinkling on South Asian chaats. It has a salty-sour flavor with hints of funk, smokiness, and heat, and it's great on fruit and vegetables. My preferred blend comes from Diaspora Co., which sources its fresh, flavorful spices from regenerative family farms.

chile (chili) crisp: This wildly popular Chinese condiment is made with a base of dried chile and oil and includes other seasonings and ingredients that vary from brand to brand. For the recipes in this book, I used Fly by Jing's basic Chili Crisp, which includes preserved black beans, garlic, sesame, Sichuan peppercorn, and other aromatics and spices. (I tend to keep their other varieties around too.)

Chinese vinegar: A variety of dark, aged vinegars are used in Chinese cooking. The most common types are Chinkiang (relatively light and tart), Shaanxi (aged and a bit richer), and Baoning (aged to varying degrees of richness, depending on how old it is). I keep all three around for different uses and as dipping sauces for dumplings.

chutneys: In South Asian cooking, "chutney" can refer to any of a variety of sauces, including the popular tamarind and mint-coriander (cilantro) versions. While these sauces are best when they're homemade, store-bought versions work fine in a pinch.

cotija: A staple of Mexican cooking, cotija is a salty, crumbly cow's-milk cheese sometimes compared to Italian ricotta salata. Cotija doesn't melt when heated, so it's often used as a garnish on dishes like elote and esquites (page 90). It's also one of the easiest Mexican cheeses to source, and is often sold in supermarkets.

douban jiang (chili bean sauce), sweet bean sauce, and hoisin sauce: These Chinese staples sometimes come in similar jars, but they have very different flavors. Douban jiang (often labeled "toban djan," for the milder kinds, or "Pixian broad bean paste," for the rich, aged kind) is a Sichuanese ingredient made of chiles and dried favas that have been fermented together. Sweet bean sauce is a sweet-savory mix of soybeans, sesame, sugar, and other ingredients; you'll often find it called "sauce for Peking duck" on the packaging. Hoisin sauce (perhaps the most common in Western markets) is a sweet-salty sauce made of fermented bean paste and flavoring ingredients like garlic and chiles; it's used to flavor moo shu dishes and to season bowls of Vietnamese pho; and, like sweet bean sauce, it can be used for Peking duck.

fried shallots: This Asian ingredient is similar to the shelf-stable fried onions you might put on an old-school American green bean casserole, but the shallots are thinner, crispier, and more flavorful. They take a lot of work to make at home, but East Asian supermarkets and online retailers sell great premade, shelf-stable versions.

furikake: Sold primarily as a seasoning for rice (or fish or vegetables), furikake is a Japanese spice mix that can include a range of ingredients, including seaweed flakes, sesame seeds, dried fish, herbs, and salt. There are many different blends out there (especially in Japanese markets), so read the ingredients list if you're looking for a specific flavor profile.

gochujang: This fermented Korean spice paste combines sweet, savory, and spicy flavors. Its mild heat and richness make it an excellent option for adding a boost to a wide variety of dishes.

injera chips: Injera—soft, chewy flatbread made from teff flour—is the base of pretty much any Ethiopian meal. But you don't always need to make the fresh stuff to enjoy injera's unique flavor. Leftover injera is traditionally left out in the sun to dry, then broken into chips; these firm, crisp shards can be used to scoop up foods like shiro mitten (page 110). You'll find the chips at Ethiopian markets.

katsuobushi: These light, papery curls and flakes of dried bonito are a staple Japanese ingredient. In restaurants, chefs shave their own using a specially designed blade, but it's a lot easier to buy a big bag of shaved katsuobushi from a Japanese market or online retailer.

Kewpie mayonnaise: This Japanese brand's mayonnaise is especially rich, because it is made with only yolks (no whites) and has added flavor from a blend of vinegars and a bit of MSG. It's the best-selling brand in Japan and is widely available in other parts of the world. Once you start using it, it will be hard to go back.

kimchi: Korean kimchi—vegetables fermented with chile paste, garlic, and other seasonings—can be made with a variety of ingredients, but the ones you'll commonly find in the market are cabbage, cucumber, and daikon. They're all fantastic, but if you want one that keeps well for a long time, grab a jar of cabbage kimchi from an artisanal producer like Mother-in-Law's.

kumquat: These tiny citrus fruits are deceptive: their skins are actually the sweet part of the fruit, while the interiors are extremely tart. They're great to eat whole— just pop them into your mouth and spit out any seeds—but they pack a punch, so I often cut them into thin slices before adding them to dishes like Unstuffed Crab and Avocado (page 128).

lemongrass: This tough, grassy herb (West Indian lemongrass, or *Cymbopogon citratus*) is a cousin of the plant used to produce citronella and has a similarly lemony, aromatic scent. It's used to flavor foods all across Southeast Asia. The leaves are not the part of the plant cooks use most; instead, they usually crush and slice (or mince) the white and light-yellow (and sometimes purple) bases of the stalk's inner leaves.

makrut lime leaves: These fragrant leaves come from the same tree as the makrut lime fruit. They are deeply fragrant, and when you mince them or slice them as thin as possible (they're pretty firm and hard to chew), they add a unique, aromatic flavor to Southeast Asian dishes or anything else you want to put them into.

Meyer lemons: These fragrant, slightly sweet lemons were first brought to the US from China in 1908 by botanist and explorer Frank Meyer; they are thought to be a cross between a lemon and some kind of orange. They used to be hard to find in Western markets (the early trees carried a virus and were banned in many places) but are now increasingly available in the US and Australia and in some markets in Europe.

miso: Salty-savory miso paste is a staple of Japanese cooking. It comes in an incredibly wide variety of flavors, but in the West the most common versions are mild shiro (white) miso, strong aka (red) miso, and medium awase miso. Shiro miso is also often labeled "Kyoto style," as it originated there and was traditionally used in food prepared for the royal family.

nori and gim: Toasted sheets of seaweed are a popular ingredient in both Japan, where they're known as nori, and Korea, where they're known as gim. The two products are very similar, but the Korean version is often sold seasoned with sesame oil and salt. Note that if you're buying nori to make hand rolls (page 65) or onigiri (page 98), you'll want to get the thicker nori sheets and not the thin, flaky styles sold in snack packs.

okonomiyaki sauce: This sweet-savory sauce (also known as okonomi sauce) is said to be related to Worcestershire sauce, but to my mind it's a bit more like an American barbecue sauce, since the primary ingredients—vinegar, tomato paste, sugar, fruit, aromatics, and spices—are quite similar. It's also used in similar ways: once you use it on Okonomiyaki Tater Tots (page 62), or on a true okonomiyaki, you can also drizzle it on anything that would benefit from a splash of rich, slightly sweet flavor.

paprika: This spice, made from dried and ground red peppers, comes in a variety of styles and is produced in a few different countries; each style has its own distinctive flavor. In these recipes I've used Spanish paprikas, which come designated "spicy," "sweet" (which is very mild), and "bittersweet" (which is in between). It can also be labeled "smoked," which means the same peppers used in other paprikas are smoked before they're ground. All are readily available and keep well in your spice rack.

pimentos: Pimentos are a variety of mild red chile pepper somewhat similar to bell pepper. My Pimento Cheese and Tomato Finger Sandwiches recipe (page 97) calls for canned pimentos, which are the same thing as the little red bits you might find inside cocktail olives.

pomegranate molasses: This sweet-tart syrup is a staple of Middle Eastern cooking. There's really no good substitute, but Western supermarkets often carry it and it's readily available online.

rice cakes: The term "rice cakes" can refer to a lot of different things, depending on where you are in the world. American rice cakes are thick, cracker-like snacks made from crispy popped rice that has been stuck together in rounds or squares. Dense, chewy Korean, Chinese, and Japanese rice cakes are a completely different kind of food, and are used in completely different ways.

rice noodles: Tender white rice noodles are a staple food all across East and Southeast Asia, especially in areas where rice is far easier to grow than wheat. Round Chinese rice noodles, often called mixian, can be hard to come by in some Western countries, but flat Vietnamese rice noodles (also sold as rice sticks) are available in many parts of the world.

roti and dosas: Frozen roti and dosas offer a quick route to dinner. Some come fully cooked and just need to be reheated; others are raw but still cook quickly on the stove or in the oven. The terms "roti" and "dosa" actually encompass a range of different styles and thicknesses, so look for the style specified in the recipe; for the Roti Pizza (page 33) you'll want a phulka- or chapati-style roti, which are quite thin.

sambal: More a category of food than a particular preparation, sambal is a style of condiment made with chiles and a wide variety of other ingredients, served in Indonesia and Malaysia. In Western countries jarred sambal oelek can be found in Asian markets and large grocery stores, and a wider variety of options can be sourced through small producers like Auria's Malaysian Kitchen and Sibeiho.

seasoned rice vinegar and mirin: These two Japanese ingredients are both often described as rice seasoning, but while they have similar uses, they have different bases and flavors. Seasoned rice vinegar is essentially white rice vinegar with salt and sugar—a mixture that many Japanese cooks make themselves but that also comes premade for convenience. It's used to season sushi rice but has a number of other uses. Mirin is a Japanese rice wine with a slightly sweet flavor (and relatively low alcohol) that is used in a variety of dishes from soups to marinades.

shiro mitten: This name applies to both the classic Ethiopian dish (page 110) and the dry mix used to make it. The mix, which is readily available at Ethiopian and African markets, combines a flour made from toasted chickpeas with all the spices that give the dish its flavor. I'm partial to the version sold in the US by Brundo Spice Company because it's incredibly fresh and is made by a small, women-led producer (and because I like its mix of ingredients and flavors).

shiso: This fresh herb, traditionally used in Japanese cooking and Chinese medicine, has a flavor that mixes notes of mint, basil, and licorice. There are two varieties—green and purple—and while they are used in different ways in Japan, they have fairly similar flavors. Shiso is often served with sushi and sashimi, so if your market doesn't have it, a good fish counter might have packages for sale.

shredded Parmesan: While I'm not usually a fan of pre-grated cheese (because it has additives, to keep it from sticking together), I make an exception for pre-shredded Parmesan, which comes in tubs in the cheese section of Western grocery stores and looks like long, thin strips (not the powder sold as "grated" Parmesan). If you don't have it, you can make something similar by using a box grater, but the pieces will be thicker and wider than store-bought.

shrimp chips: These crispy, crunchy rounds (also sold as prawn crisps or shrimp snacks) are made of tapioca starch and shrimp meat. They're often associated with Thai restaurants, where they might be served at the start of a meal, but you can buy them in bags, like potato chips, in many Asian markets and through online retailers.

Sichuan pepper oil: Sichuan pepper, or peppercorns (actually the husks of the berries of the Chinese prickly ash tree), have a mild citrusy flavor, but they are best known for producing a tingling, numbing sensation when eaten. This oil offers an easy way to add that flavor and tingle to pretty much any type of food. The quality of the oils available in Western markets has improved exponentially in the past few years; my favorites come from specialists like the company 50Hertz, which offers both oils made with red peppercorns (with a relatively warm, balanced flavor) and green peppercorns (with a slightly stronger, brasher flavor).

soy sauce: While this ingredient has become ubiquitous in most countries around the world, some cooks may be surprised to learn that there are actually a few varieties of the stuff available, each with its own qualities. Japanese soy sauces come in a few different styles, but the most common version in the West, shoyu (the kind sold by Kikkoman), is relatively dark and strong. Chinese soy sauces primarily come in two strengths: light, which has a lighter flavor than the Japanese variety, and dark, which is thick and sticky and a little bit sweet. If you don't have Chinese light soy sauce, you can use the Japanese variety, but start with one-third to one-half of the amount indicated in the recipe, then adjust as needed.

sriracha: This chile sauce has its origins in Thailand, but the slightly thick version found in Western stores is primarily made by a Vietnamese company that adapted the sauce decades ago. It's a great way to add flavorful, relatively mild heat to pretty much anything; the exact flavor of the mixture varies by brand.

Turkish pepper paste: Made from sweet peppers (and sometimes a few spicy ones, to add some very mild heat), this ingredient is also called biber salçası. It's used in a variety of ways in Turkish cooking and adds a deep, rich flavor to all kinds of dishes. It's readily available in Middle Eastern markets and through online retailers, but if you can't find it, you can substitute tomato paste with a pinch of ground dried chile.

Velveeta: This American processed cheese is specifically engineered to melt well; it's the key ingredient in queso, a Tex-Mex classic. In Australia, you might find Velveeta labeled as Kraft Cheddar Cheese; in other parts of the world, you'll have to find an American market to get it (except, apparently, in South Korea, Panama, and the Philippines, where it's pretty popular).

Vietnamese fish sauce: Used throughout Southeast Asia, fish sauce adds rich, salty, umami-heavy flavor to all kinds of foods. Different countries and regions use different kinds of seafood to make the sauce, so the style you buy will have a significant impact on the finished flavors of your dish. I rely primarily on Vietnamese-style fish sauce because it's readily available in the West and is milder than its Thai cousin.

Vietnamese rice paper: This Vietnamese staple is so popular all around the world that you're likely to find it in many Western supermarkets (and, of course, in Asian supermarkets and online). The sheets are very hard and feel thick in their dried state, but a quick soak in cool water will make them pliable and a bit sticky.

yuzu kosho: This Japanese condiment, made primarily from spicy chile peppers and yuzu citrus fruit, packs a strong punch and a lot of bright flavor. It's great on anything that could benefit from a really bright, floral citrus note and some good heat, and it's often added to dressings and sauces or used to enliven meat and fish dishes. A little goes a long way, so a small jar will last a while.

za'atar: This wildly popular seasoning blend—made of dried oregano, thyme, and marjoram; sesame seeds; and, often, sumac—is used in countless Middle Eastern dishes. It's also readily available from a number of Western spice companies. Every company makes a slightly different version, so taste the mixture before adding additional sumac, salt, or other ingredients.

ACKNOWLEDGMENTS

It took a small army of dedicated and enthusiastic friends, family members, and snack lovers to bring this book to life. First and foremost, I am incredibly grateful to my publisher/editor, Jenny Wapner, and my agent, Danielle Svetcov, who both saw the potential in this idea and provided invaluable enthusiasm and collaboration as the book grew and took shape.

I feel both lucky and grateful to have worked with all the wonderful chefs and cooks who shared their time and recipes with me—and allowed me to share their foods with you: Nafy Flatley, Jing Gao and the team at Fly by Jing, Nora Haron, Steve Joo, Matthew Meyer, Sachiko Ormsby, Pervaiz Shallwani, and Daniel Aderaw Yeshiwas and Jess Anthony plus the rest of the team at Cafe Colucci and Brundo Spice Company. This book would not have been nearly as rich (or as fun to work on) without your ideas and input.

I also feel blessed to have worked with photographer and stylist Leela Cyd, and her team—David Kilpatrick, Liza Saragosa, Becky Sue Wilberding, and Jasmine Shimoda—who helped bring all these recipes to life and make them even more beautiful than I could have imagined.

This project also couldn't have come to fruition without the help of my volunteer recipe testers: Betsy Andrews, Dena Beard, Christine Bell, Vered Ben Gideon, Catherine Martin Christopher, Devra Ferst, Rendy Freedman, Susan Bacon Fredrickson, Christine Gallary, Erin Gleeson, Lea Fredrickson Hemsing, Hilary Ingoldsby, Hilary Jacks, Leah Koenig, Deborah Kwan, Andre Lazar and Haley Smith, Ashlyn Clark McCague, Janet McKracken, Tracie McMillan, Sita Raiter, Katie Sapp, Peter Tittman and Malia Wollan, Hannah Freedman Wagner, Barbara Wand, and Annelies Zijderveld.

My sincerest thanks to the entire team at Hardie Grant, including Carolyn Insley, Liz Correll, Natalie Lundgren, Maddy Kalmowitz, publicist Stephanie Moon, and book designer Ashley Lima.

Last but not least, my deepest gratitude to my wonderful family, Josh and Nora, for their love and support and for putting up with the months when I took over our kitchen for my work, my obsession with all things snack-related, and some unorthodox meal planning.

INDEX

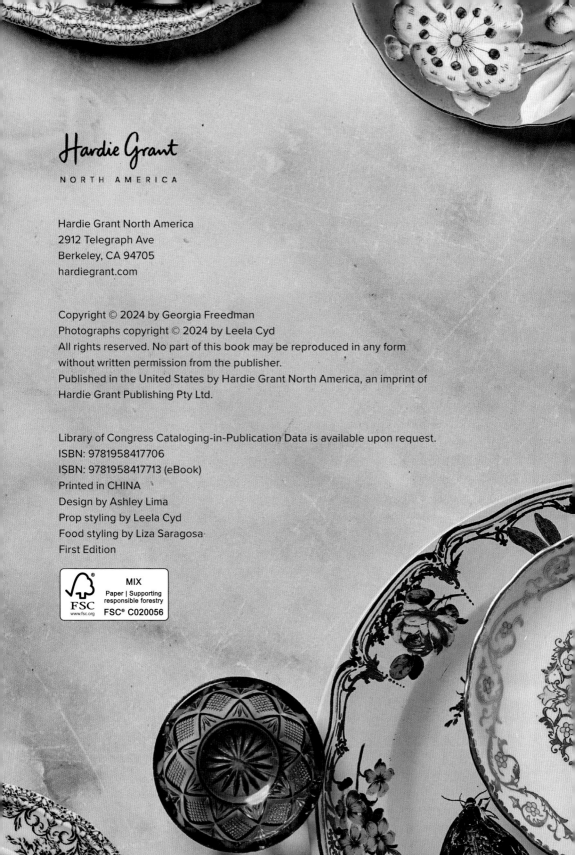

Hardie Grant

NORTH AMERICA

Hardie Grant North America
2912 Telegraph Ave
Berkeley, CA 94705
hardiegrant.com

Published in the United States by Hardie Grant North America, an imprint of
Hardie Grant Publishing Pty Ltd.

Library of Congress Cataloging-in-Publication Data is available upon request.
ISBN: 9781958417706
ISBN: 9781958417713 (eBook)
Printed in CHINA
Design by Ashley Lima
Prop styling by Leela Cyd
Food styling by Liza Saragosa
First Edition